Abandonment of the Patient

Ellen D. Baer, RN, PhD, FAAN, is a Visiting Professor of Nursing at New York University, where she is director of the nursing doctoral program. She also is Professor Emerita of Nursing at the University of Pennsylvania, where she held the Hillman Term Professorship in Nursing, was one of the founding members of the Center for the Study of the History of Nursing, and remains an associate Director of the Center. She has published and spoken widely on nursing subjects. In recognition of her work, Dr. Baer received the 1988 Lavinia Dock Award from the American Association for the History of Nursing, the 1990 Distinguished Nurse Researcher Award from the Foundation of the New York State Nurses Association, the 1992 Media Award from the American Academy of Nursing, and the Centennial Nursing Heritage Award from the American Nurses' Association in 1996.

In the last 2 years, Dr. Baer has focused her energy on alerting the public to the dangers of hospital restructuring, replacement of nurses with untrained aides, and the negative impact of these changes on quality patient care. In addition to speaking widely about her concerns, Dr. Baer has co-authored, with Suzanne Gordon, several op-ed essays on the topic, which have appeared in *The New York Times, The Boston Globe, The Los Angeles Times,* and *The Philadelphia Inquirer.*

Claire M. Fagin, RN, PhD, FAAN, is the Leadership Professor and Dean Emerita of the University of Pennsylvania, School of Nursing. Dean of the School of Nursing from 1977–1992, she served as Interim President of the University of Pennsylvania from 1993–1994. Dr. Fagin's 40 years of progressive experience in nursing, health care, and educational administration have blended an interest in consumer health issues with professional health and nursing issues. As a researcher, educator, and administrator Dr. Fagin has been an advocate of lowering health care costs for the consumer and providing Americans with research-based health services. She is known for her work on nursing's cost effectiveness and her efforts with consumers and health professionals to create a new paradigm for access and quality. Her most recent work was a study on nursing home reform.

Dr. Fagin is a member of the Institute of Medicine, National Academy of Sciences, and of its Board of Health Promotion and Disease Prevention; the Expert Panel on Nursing of the World Health Organization, and the American Academy of Arts and Sciences. She received the Honorary Recognition Award of the American Nurses Association, the most prestigious honor awarded in the nursing profession, in June 1988. Among her other awards are the first Distinguished Scholar Award and the Hildegard E. Peplau Award for her work in psychiatric nursing, from the American Nurses Association.

Suzanne Gordon is a freelance journalist and author. She is the author of five books and a frequent contributor to *The Boston Globe* and the *Los Angeles Times* op-ed page. She has written for *The New York Times, The Washington Post, The Philadelphia Inquirer, The Atlantic Monthly, Harper's, Ms., The Nation,* and many other major publications.

Ms. Gordon writes about women's issues, health care, and nursing. She has just completed a major book on nursing to be published by Little Brown and Co. in 1996. The book is titled *Nurses: The Story of Three RN's, Their Patients, and a Health Care System That Undervalues Care.* Her articles on nursing have won awards from The American Academy of Nursing, The American Association of Critical Care Nurses, The Massachusetts Organization of Nurse Executives and the University of Massachusetts (Boston) College of Nursing. For her writing illuminating the work of caregivers Ms. Gordon was awarded an honorary doctorate form Fitchburg State College.

Abandonment of the Patient

*The Impact of Profit-Driven
Health Care on the Public*

Ellen D. Baer
Claire M. Fagin
Suzanne Gordon

Editors

SPRINGER PUBLISHING COMPANY

Copyright © 1996 Springer Publishing Company, Inc.

Springer Publishing Company, Inc.
536 Broadway
New York, NY 10012-3955

Second Printing

97 98 99 00 / 5 4 3 2

Library of Congress Cataloging-in-Publication Data

Abandonment of the patient : the impact of profit-driven health care on
  the public / Ellen D. Baer, Claire M. Fagin, Suzanne Gordon,
  editors.
      p.   cm.
  Includes bibliographical references and index.
  ISBN 0-8261-9470-2
    1. Managed care plans (Medical care)—United States.   2. Medical
economics—United States.   I. Baer, Ellen Davidson.   II. Fagin,
Claire M.   III. Gordon, Suzanne, 1945–
    [DNLM: 1. Quality of Health Care—trends—United States.
2. Delivery of Health Care—trends—United States.   3. Delivery of
Health Care—economics—United States.   4. Managed Care Programs—
United States.   W 84 AA1 A11 1996]
  RA413.A23   1996
  362.1'0973—dc20
  DNLM/DLC   96-2719
  for Library of Congress   CIP

Printed in the United States of America

It may seem a strange principle to enunciate
as the very first requirement in a hospital
that it should do the sick no harm.

Florence Nightingale
Notes on Hospitals, 1859

Contents

Contributors

Hilary Abramson is a journalist and former patient from San Francisco, California.

Eloise Balasco is Vice President for Nursing at Mercy Hospital in Portland, Maine.

Sidney D. Blumenthal is Special Political Correspondent for the New Yorker Magazine, from Washington, D. C.

Arthur Caplan is Trustee Professor of Bioethics and Director of the Center for Bioethics at the University of Pennsylvania, in Philadelphia, Pennsylvania.

Clark E. Kerr is President of ConsumerFirst in Danville, California.

Joan E. Lynaugh is Professor, Associate Dean and Director of Graduate Education at the School of Nursing at the University of Pennsylvania, in Philadelphia, Pennsylvania.

John O'Brien is Administrator and Chief Executive Officer of the Cambridge Hospital in Cambridge, Massachusetts.

John M. O'Donnell is Director of the Surgical Intensive Care Unit and Chairman of the Department of Surgical Critical Care at the Lahey Clinic-Hitchcock Medical Center in Burlington, Massachusetts.

J. Sanford Schwartz is the Robert D. Eilers Professor of Medicine and Health Management and Economics at the School of Medicine and in the Wharton School, and executive director of the Leonard Davis Institute of Health Economics at the University of Pennsylvania, Philadelphia, Pennsylvania.

Janie Storr is a registered nurse at Providence Hospital in Seattle, Washington.

Ann Torragrossa is Director of the Pennsylvania Health Law Project in Philadelphia, Pennsylvania.

Bruce C. Vladeck is the Administrator of the Health Care Financing Administration of the Department of Health and Human Services of the United States of America.
Quentin D. Young is Clinical Professor of Preventative Medicine at the University of Illinois Medical Center and senior attending physician at Michael Reese Hospital in Chicago, Illinois.

Preface

Over the past 3 years, all three of the editors of this book have observed the enormous changes occurring in the health care field—often at the expense of patient care. Because of their articles in lay journals (1994; 1995), Suzanne Gordon and Ellen Baer, in particular, found themselves on the listening end of numerous phone calls from physicians, nurses, and patients regarding their experiences. Our shared concerns caused us to take constructive steps to highlight our concerns and develop strategies to improve health care conditions in the future. This led to the organization of a symposium on the Abandonment of the Patient, which took place in December 1995, Philadelphia. It was sponsored by the Leadership Lecture Fund of the University of Pennsylvania School of Nursing. This book is derived from that symposium.

We intend this book to be a wake-up call to the American public about the current realities of the health care system, which are increasingly characterized by cost-cutting and profit, rather than quality care in a cost-effective modality. Among the contributing authors are physicians, nurses, patients, lawyers, journalists, administrators, and ethicists.

We hope the book will serve as a stimulus to health care professionals, concerned journalists, and the lay public to seek information and press for actions that will safeguard and improve health, individually and collectively, in our nation.

Introduction

Claire Fagin

This book considers one of the most critical issues we face as a nation—the abandonment of the sick and vulnerable in an increasingly cost cutting, market-driven health care system. Several years ago a trickle of reports from nurses, physicians, and patients began to suggest that some hospitals' versions of restructuring and reengineering were compromising the care that patients were receiving. We watched the downsizing that was occurring in nursing and other clinical staff in hospitals, often irrespective of patient acuity and occupancy, and we started to hear about dreadful events related to the higher patient loads nurses were carrying, the replacement of nurses by unlicensed, barely trained personnel, and by the tensions felt by front-line personnel caused by the sea change occurring in health care.

However, problems in hospitals are only one piece of the story. We have come to realize that the problems are much broader and will permeate all aspects of health care, and affect people of all ages and income levels. Current Congressional plans for Medicare and Medicaid conflated by managed care initiatives will lead to cost shifting that will create impossible burdens for American businesses and families. Whether you are insured

1

or uninsured, if you are sick you will have to fight for health care. You will have to fight to see a physician, you will have to fight to see a nurse practitioner for primary care and preventive services, and you will have to really fight to see a specialist.

If patients are hospitalized for major illnesses, operations, or other procedures, they will have to fight to stay in the hospital to get needed nursing and medical care, and they probably won't succeed, with tragic consequences for many. For many hospitals, even in the not-for-profit world, the concern about competition and managed care cost imperatives has resulted not only in the shortest length of hospital stays in the industrialized world, but in massive reduction in expert nursing staff in almost all hospitals in the country—and it is only just beginning.

Just look at the statistics. According to a study done in conjunction with the American Hospital Association's *Hospitals & Health Networks* magazine (Cerne, 1994), three-fourths of American hospitals are engaged in or developing plans for restructuring. Restructuring as a word and as a concept is just fine—like managed care—exactly what we need. However, restructuring has come to be seen as the hiring of high-priced consultants or new short-lived administrators whose principal method for cutting costs is to replace RNs—who represent a paltry 23 percent of hospital wages—with "patient care assistants." In many hospitals these barely trained people now give bedside care to patients who are more acutely ill than ever before. It is unconscionable that the changes in nursing care staff are much higher than in any other group employed by the hospital.

The recent publicized deaths and morbidities occurring in hospitals in Boston, Florida, New York, and Michigan (among others), seemed to be related to major changes in hospital organization, including downsizing of the nursing staff and changes in their responsibilities away from direct patient care. Based on my own personal observations, I believe we are entering a new experience. One where the actual nursing shortage of the 1980s is being created artificially by deliberate downsizing of nursing staffs irrespective of patient occupancy and need. This can only have dire results for the abandoned patient.

So how has all this happened so quickly? Briefly put, these changes are a result of a conflation of concerns and responses: The American public's concerns about the cost of coverage and lack of coverage; the concern of business about their huge health benefits bills; the promises of for-profit managed care organizations to fill the gap at a price; congressional proposals to sharply reduce increases in Medicare and Medicaid; and the efforts of cash-hungry, capital-intensive hospitals to build surpluses. A Madison Avenue approach to quality patient care has become the norm in a very short time-frame. With the cuts in care, we are seeing accumulations of wealth in the health care field that are unprecedented. In a massive transfer of wealth, the money that HMOs save by denying care to working people, even middle-class professionals who have health insurance, is being redirected to the incomes of the for-profit executives and large corporate shareholders. No wonder the cover of *Modern Health Care* trumpeted, "We're In The Money" (Lutz & Pallarito, 1995). It also told us that the very hospitals that say they are too poor to pay the salaries of expert nurses, laboratory technicians, social workers, and others are sitting on the largest cash reserves in their history.

It's ironic that Nursing's Agenda for Health Care Reform (1991), which I and other colleagues helped write, relied on Managed Care as the modality of the future to serve all Americans in a universal system of accessible, coordinated care, which would be consumer driven, outcome based, and fully disclosed. However, what corporate America now refers to as "managed care" is really a competitive system to manage costs and contraverts many of the principles undergirding actual management of care. Thus, it is important to distinguish between the two, and when referring to the actual management of care, we must say that precisely.

This book does not represent any one profession or group. The authors that have shared their insights and experiences with us in the book come from across the nation and represent a wide spectrum of America with interests in the health care arena. They not only write from their heads—to analyze the situation we are living today—but from their hearts. Many of the issues that doctors and nurses and patients and social workers face have been conveniently dismissed by either industry leaders, politicians, or, sadly, members of the media. Doctors are said to be complaining because the corporate version of managed care will hurt their incomes. Nurses like Janie Storr, or nursing administrators like Eloise Balasco, who worry about their inability to deliver quality or safe care in hospitals, are accused of complaining to "protect their jobs." Administrators of public hospitals, like John O'Brien, are said to care for only a small segment of the American population—the poor. The experiences of patients who offer their stories, like Hilary Abramson, are discarded because they are only isolated cases. The doctors, nurses, administrators, ethicists, journalists, and patients whose chapters follow offer us a view, not of a microcosm, but of the macrocosm of what is becoming the rule in health care.

No one involved in this book is in favor of a return to the days when patients stayed in hospitals for weeks on end, when the health care system focused only on the aggressive treatment of acute illnesses, and when physicians were free to recommend treatment without regard to cost. But we are in favor of protesting a version of health care reform that so radically redefines the morality of health care and those who provide it.

It is clear that all of us believe that an alarm is necessary to wake up the American public to the dangers all around us in an industry we have all trusted to "do no harm." We invite readers to share our concern, to advance the process of public education about the real purposes of health care, and to brainstorm and strategize about how we use the momentum of the current situation to create the kind of health care system we need.

PART I

The Setting for Health Care Change

—— *Introduction by J. Sanford Schwartz* ——

When I was in Hebrew School, we studied a book of sayings called "Pirke Avot: Sayings of the Fathers." In it there was a quote that said, "Pray for the government and your leaders because without them, men will destroy each other." Never have the challenges for leadership at the national level been more necessary or more in demand than they are today. We are extremely fortunate in this country to have Bruce Vladeck, who writes the chapter that follows, as the director of the Health Care Financing Administration—the part of the government that has primary responsibility for ensuring the health of three of the most vulnerable populations in society: the elderly, the disabled, and the poor. While it's never been good to be poor, this is a particularly bad time to be poor in this country.

Dr. Vladeck was an assistant vice president at the Robert Wood Johnson Foundation, where he helped shape the national health services and policy research agenda. At Robert Wood Johnson, he contributed to some of the most creative thinking about what health care ought to be and how it should be examined in an effective fashion.

In the early 1980s, he became New Jersey's Assistant Commissioner for Health, and established the DRG (Diagnostic Related Groups) system in New Jersey. Not only did he establish a DRG system which was well before its time in recognizing the need to provide high-quality medical care in an efficient way, but he had the foresight to combine this with the all-payor system. Dr. Vladeck recognized that even under so-called economic or market models, there will be a need to adjust, correct, and regulate the market where the market will not work. While many of the good components of the New Jersey DRG program were adopted, when it was generalized or extrapolated to the national level, the all-payor system unfortunately was not. We would not be having some of the allocative and distributive problems to the underserved we do today at the national level if we had adopted the all-payor system.

Dr. Vladeck also brings a great deal of other experience to HCFA. He was president of the New York Hospital Fund, and has been on the boards of the Henry J. Kaiser Foundation and the New York Health and Hospital Corporation. His challenge now, and the perspective from which he has written his chapter, is as administrator of the Health Care Financing Administration.

In his book *Equity and Efficiency: The Big Tradeoff* (1975), Arthur Okun, of the Brookings Institution, identified the inherent fundamental tension that exists in American society between a belief in productivity and efficiency on the one hand, and the need to balance such efficiency concerns with the fundamental, egalitarian democratic basis of our society on the other. These conflicting forces are currently being debated throughout society, and it is an enormous challenge in health care in particular.

Dr. Bruce Vladeck has been providing intelligence, vision, and leadership in addressing these challenges in Washington, and this is reflected in the chapter you are about to read.

CHAPTER 1

The Corporatization of American Health Care and Why It Is Happening

Bruce C. Vladeck

It is clear that we are in a period of extreme turmoil in the health care system. What I like to tell some of the more enthusiastic advocates and beneficiaries of the recent changes is that the one thing we can say for certain about revolutions is that you never really know quite how they will turn out. The other thing about revolutions is that the cost of living through them is significant for everyone involved.

There are a number of things going on that are extremely disturbing to people. There are also a number of things going on that hold out some very important promises.

The phrase "corporatization of health care" is a useful phrase to capture some of the consolidation going on in the health system. Large publicly traded corporations are increasingly important actors in the health scene and, perhaps more importantly, are having an effect on communities, on patients, and on health care professionals. If you look at the phenomenon of corporatization, there are positives and negatives.

We really have only two choices before us as a society in terms of health care. We can significantly increase the productivity of our health care system by providing better outcomes and higher-quality services for less cost in real resource terms. Or, we will have to add a much more formal and mechanistic rationing system to the implicit and class-based rationing that has always existed in our health care system.

Three things are important to consider. First is the issue of basic demographics. Second is the lower rates of long-term economic growth. Third is the fact that the more we look at efforts to cut back on services, the more we realize how many health care needs we were not meeting even when we were flush. Many people continue to be underserved, a condition that existed even before the era of cost containment and corporatization. All of this means that even if society could afford to maintain the historical rate of growth and the amount of resources being added in the health sector, it could not continue to do so indefinitely.

To that extent, making the health care system significantly more productive is a moral imperative, given the intrinsic moral unacceptability of formally rationing services, and the even less desirable ethical status of the informal and indirect ways in which we currently ration the availability of services. In this regard, there is something to be said for some of the things happening in the name of corporatization of the American health care system.

There's a lot of integration of health care delivery systems going on in the name of corporatization. A good deal of this integration is all form and no substance. Much of it has to do with buying and selling, or the development and the closing of a variety of provider organizations, generally defined and constructed primarily in the interest of maximizing Medicare reimbursement. These are gathered under some kind of common ownership or control, without any serious effort to integrate the services or patient care across the various component parts. Nonetheless, in these institutions, both for-profit and not-for-profit, some are taking the notion of an integrated delivery system seriously. We have all known for a long time that there were very significant potential benefits for patients and clinicians alike from being able to keep a primary care giver. We know it is useful to have a broader range of services under one roof rather than having to bounce the patient back and forth among various sites, for the convenience of the caregiver. We know it is beneficial to have the simple integration of medical records and elimination of duplicative information-gathering and so forth.

To the extent that integration of delivery systems is real—although it may occur in only a small fraction of the so-called integrated systems—there are significant benefits. There should be, as well, significant economies. As in the corporate, manufacturing, or service sector, it ought to be possible to reduce input costs for the production of particular kinds of health services by re-engineering the ways in which we do things, by working smarter not harder.

Certainly, there is much irrational downsizing going on in the health care business, just as there has been in manufacturing and private service corporations. It is extremely difficult to make the argument, though, that the typical American hospital or, indeed, even the traditional American outpatient or long-term-care facility was, prior to the recent wave of efforts at downsizing and greater efficiency, a model of the way to run an organization.

Here is an illustration. About two and a half years ago, a very close friend of ours who is a senior administrator at one of the great teaching hospitals in New York City, tried to schedule some social events with us. She explained to us that she was going to have to change her plans because the nurses in her hospital were planning a strike and, as management, not only did she have to be available for fill-in duty during the strike, but she needed some retraining since she hadn't done clinical work in a number of years. She had been assigned to critical care units, which she hadn't done for three or four years, and needed a serious refresher course. This friend had gotten out of clinical nursing, in part, to go back to school to get another degree so she could become an administrator.

I asked her what the institution's plans were in terms of delaying elective admissions and otherwise cutting back on operations during the strike. She said that the expectation was that the strike would last only a few days, and there were no plans for such a reduction. I said that really seemed to be pushing the edge of the envelope very hard. No, she explained that if the strike lasted only a week, they would actually have more R.N.s on the floor than on normal staffing patterns, because there were so many who were working in nonclinical care jobs in that institution that they could staff three shifts for a week more fully than when they were operating on a regular basis.

Now, I don't know how typical this institution was. It was one that we thought of in the New York environment as being particularly efficient and well managed. But if you look at the data from Himmelstein and Woolhandler (1994), for example, as to what happened in staffing American hospitals during the 1980s, you see this enormous growth in nonservice-delivery middle management in nursing. In other parts of departments occupied or staffed largely by professional nurses, and in financial management and other parts of the organizations, this is true as well.

This looks very much like what happened to General Motors or Ford or Chrysler in the 1960s and to other corporations, some of which are still with us, and some of which aren't. Or consider the experience of our own organization, the Health Care Financing Administration—which, by any standards other than those of certain ideologues, was not a highly overstaffed organization to begin with. We have reduced the number of managerial positions in our organization in the last eighteen months by 50 percent, and the agency is working substantially better as a result.

The fact is, there is a lot of thoughtless activity that goes on in the name of downsizing. There are many organizations that cut costs by cutting short-term cost. The simple fact of the matter is that, if we are going to be able to provide high-quality health care to the American public in the next century, we have to be substantially more efficient and productive in the way we deliver health care than we are now.

I drive an American-built automobile that is of substantially higher quality than the car I had ten years ago, and it was produced with half as many person-hours of labor as the car I purchased ten years ago. Some of that is due to technological change. Some of that is because we build cars in this country in an entirely different way than we used to.

We are in the process of running governments in an entirely different way than we used to run governments, and we are going to have to operate the health care system in an entirely different way, as well.

In principle, it is very hard to argue with notions of continuity of care, with a single point of contact, with case managers, with access to not only the full range of specialists, but a full range of ancillary services, and a uniform patient record. It is also hard to argue with viewing the delivery of health services in the context of a financial and information base that looks at the health of a population over time, rather than the management of particular acute interventions.

There is no question that the literature is very clear and the examples today are very clear of instances in which managed care organizations, both not-for-profit and for-profit, are living up to at least some of the potential contained in those principles. It doesn't always happen. Perhaps it has been happening increasingly less often than it did in the past.

However, when I talk to the managers of the old traditional nonprofit HMOs that have been historically identified with a high quality of care, and around whom the public enthusiasm about HMOs developed over the last 20 years, they say that for the first time in their organizational history, the competition with their new competitors who are less interested than they are with the quality of care and long-term well-being of patients, is forcing them to rethink the ways in which they do business. They are deciding, in fact, that there are a lot of things they could do a lot better than they did in the past, as well.

Corporatization has brought with it a market for data-driven decision-making processes of one sort or another. It has created the beginnings of a movement towards reorganizing the way we do business around the capture, maintenance, and use of clinically relevant, accurate data. It has also encouraged the development of testable empirically based benchmarks, clinical pathways, and outcome measures for performance, both of individual providers of services and for systems of care.

All of us with backgrounds or involvement in health services research have been arguing for this for the last 20 or 25 years. It is starting to happen. It is starting to happen because of the economic and organizational pressures in the health care system. And we are finally beginning to see some of its results.

Finally, the most effective corporations in the health care system, like the most effective corporations in any other line of work, have brought into the health care system in this country over the last decade something that is still largely lacking in health care systems in the rest of the world. Something that was historically lacking in the health care system in the United States—a commitment to systematically talking to and listening to patients about what they want out of the health care system. There is a customer focus in the smartest and most effective corporations of all kinds which contrasts very dramatically with traditional mores of ''the professional knows best.''

The broader mores of society, our feelings about authority, our willingness to defer to holders of positions of authority has changed radically throughout society in the last generation or two. It is, in fact, a fundamentally different form of organizational behavior to try to find out, in systematic ways, the preferences, desires, needs, anxieties, wants, and concerns of your customers. Quite often you will find they are not identical to what you have assumed they are.

Here is one illustration of how this can be done. In the mid-1980s, I was fortunate to be a member of the Committee on Nursing Home Regulation of the Institute of Medicine (IOM, 1986), which wrote a comprehensive report on nursing home regulation. This became the basis of the Nursing Home Reform Act of 1987, which has had remarkably positive effects on the quality of nursing home care in the United States. For some mysterious reason, the Congress is now seeking, in effect, to repeal it.

One of the major contributions of that report and one of the major changes in the law was that we totally redesigned the way we inspect or survey long-term care facilities. We do it around the really radical notion that when a surveyor goes into a facility to try to evaluate the quality of care, one way to gain information is to ask the patients about their perceptions on the quality of care. To do this, we ask some relatively straightforward and structured questions. I will confess that I was one of the real skeptics on the committee about the potential utility of that approach.

I was familiar with the data that showed a third to a half of all nursing home residents suffered from significant cognitive impairment of one kind or another. I was very familiar with the problems of the fear of intimidation or coercion on the part of nursing home residents and their families. I was very skeptical about the ability to develop the kinds of instruments one would need to train surveyors to elicit from residents that sort of information in an effective and reliable way.

But, in fact, refocusing our definition of quality of care and how we measure it in nursing homes around what patients, in part, tell us, is the core of the real revolution in the quality of services in nursing homes in the United States. We have had such surprising good luck with it that we are beginning to extend the same model to all of our facility surveys and all of our quality measurements in health care.

John Ware (Stewart & Ware, 1992) has demonstrated, to a remarkable degree, that if you want to know about the quality of health care people are getting, the simplest and most cost-effective way to do it is to ask them. You must not ask them only at one point in time, but ask them over a period of time, using instruments that you keep refining in terms of validity. For too long, the traditional health care system in this country assumed that doctor knew best, or administrator knew best, or nurse knew best. Now we are in the process of really changing the way we do business, and I think the pressures of what we call corporatization have a lot to do with it.

Whatever the source, it is fundamentally a very healthy change in health care. On the other hand, it is clear that one of the things that is wrong with American corporations these days is that we increasingly manage most corporations in the United States, including those in the health care business, not on a long-term basis, but on a quarter-to-quarter basis.

The more we compensate high-level managers of corporations with stock or stock equivalents in their corporations and the more the market responds with increasing volatility to short-term expectations about the performance of corporations of all kinds, the more we see behavior oriented toward short-term profit maximization at the potential expense of the long-term well-being of the corporation. There are horror stories of that sort about corporations of all kinds throughout the economy. So too there are stories about health care corporations. But, in health care, this kind of short-term as opposed to long-term focus is particularly baleful and damaging. It is damaging not only to the corporations which engage in it, but to their patients and the providers of health services as well.

Much of what works best and makes the health care system most productive does involve investment over a period of time in preventive services and behavioral change. It demands the management of chronic conditions of one kind or another that simply can't be accomplished in a short time span.

Second, the core of effective health care is still the development of strong relationships between patients and caregivers. This implies continuity, and repeated and continual interchange over a period of time—precisely what people focused on the very short term can't afford or can't permit.

An extreme example of this comes when we no longer talk about patients or customers, but lives, which are bought and sold in some parts of the managed care market. We see this when the turnover in ownership of particular plans or particular organizations has been particularly rapid. We see it when people find themselves in different health care systems from one month to the next—due to a set of financial transactions that are totally disconnected from any clinical care or delivery of services. This often creates actual disruption in care.

There is also the increased turnover in the corporate side of health care. To take the example I know best, the market share, as defined by either beds, inpatient beds, or revenues, of for-profit publicly owned hospital corporations in the United States has been roughly constant for about 30 years. Those of you who have been in the business long enough realize that all of the leading corporations in the general hospital business in the United States are new players, who have entered the business within the last decade, because the short-termers in the previous business got out of it.

Similarly, the proportion of nursing homes in the United States operated on a for-profit basis has been almost constant for 20 years. The proportion of nursing homes owned by multifacility corporations has increased very significantly over that time, as has the concentration of ownership in relatively fewer multifacility corporations. But, there again, the market leaders are a somewhat different cast of characters than was the case just a few short years ago.

Because of a series of decisions made by my predecessor, an extraordinary proliferation of for-profit home care agencies in the United States has occurred over the last decade. There has been a significant corporatization of home care. Again, the total market share of the for-profit part of the industry has not grown very dramatically. In fact, there is actually some stasis in the share that the big national corporations own. But there is a lot of buying and selling, changes in management, and instability. That instability filters down to the level of clinical services in ways that have very significant disruptive and adverse effects on people's health care.

We must also consider that our perceptions of effective modern corporations run counter to certain realities. No matter how modern and sophisticated and knowledgeable we get, health care markets and services seem increasingly locally based. To quote Steve Shortell, a documenter of the corporatization of health care, there is an increasing realization that caring for a population is best done within a defined geographic regional market and that management and government structures are probably best located at these sites (Shortell et al., 1990, 1994).

This may be one of the reasons why the total proportion of the health care system under essentially national ownership is not changing that dramatically. What we are seeing are corporations based at the local and regional level increasingly imitating, for a variety of reasons and for a variety of purposes, national corporations which aren't real threats or potential competitors to them. Most importantly, corporate providers of health care, like corporate providers of anything else, provide services of varying degrees of accessibility and quality to people who have the ability to participate in the market.

But, health care is a peculiar market in many ways. Perhaps the most peculiar way is the systematic correlation between the need of people for health care and their inability to purchase it with their own resources. In this society, the younger you are and the wealthier you are, the healthier you are, and vice versa. Therefore, the great majority of medical care in many communities in the United States is bought on behalf of the folks who need that care, but who can't get it if left to their own resources. The arithmetic is very simple.

We provide health insurance through Medicare and Medicaid for just over a quarter of the population of the United States, which accounts for just about 35 to 40 percent of the health care spending in the United States. That's not because we're government and inherently inefficient. On the contrary, on a service-for-service basis, we actually buy almost everything more cheaply than the private sector does. But the folks for whom we provide coverage are more expensive and harder to care for than the folks who either individually or through their employers have private health insurance. Within private health insurance markets, the younger and healthier members of a group use substantially less health care than the older and less well-educated.

We are also rapidly increasing the number of Americans with no access to the health care system at all because they don't have health insurance, can't afford it, and can't get it. We are adding to the number of uninsured in this country at the net rate of about a hundred thousand people a month, and this is in a period of historically low unemployment and reasonably good economic growth.

One of the things that began to happen in the 1980s, for the first time since health insurance became widespread in this country in the 1930s, was that the number of uninsured people went up while the economy was going up. The number of uninsured people went up dramatically more during the recession of the late 1980s, and it never recovered as the economy recovered; and goodness knows what will happen in the next recession.

On top of that, Congress has passed legislation, which we project would eliminate health insurance for 8 million people in the Medicaid program over the next 7 years. This would roughly double the rate of growth in the uninsured population. And this is a relatively conservative estimate.

In fact, if you look at the data, one of the reasons the average member of the public is not as aware as he or she should be of what is happening to health insurance in this country is because, since 1988 there are about 7 million fewer people with private health insurance. At the same time there are about 5 million more people with Medicaid. Now, they are not the same people in a one-for-one kind of ratio, but the availability of Medicaid has, to some extent, concealed from people's awareness what is going on in the private health insurance market.

This has been going on in the private health insurance market during a period of relatively strong economic growth and substantial gains in performance. Yet, as today's political debate reveals, we cannot sustain the rates of growth in cost that those programs have experienced over the last couple of decades—in terms of the long-term well-being and financial solvency of the Medicare program, and of the federal budget and of states who share with us the cost of the Medicaid program.

No curve can go up at these rates indefinitely. The revenue sources with which we have to pay for services are not growing nearly as fast as the demands on the programs, and are never going to grow as quickly as they grew in the past. This means that we have to find a way to capture, learn from, and benefit from the good side of the transformation and corporatization of health care.

We have to learn good lessons about increased productivity, systems building, and services integration. We have to learn how to distinguish high-quality managed care under capitated arrangements, from poor-quality managed care. We have to encourage the development of more good-quality managed care and drive the poor-quality managed care out of the market.

We need to build more competition into the way in which we run our programs. In the public programs, we must benefit from competition on the basis not only of price, but of quality and customer satisfaction. We are going to have to go further than the most aggressive and ambitious of the modern corporations in demanding that everyone who participates in the health care system participate in the provision, checking, and maintenance of very high-quality data. And this data must be used to change the way services are provided and care is given.

The fact of the matter is that there has been, over a period of many years, a qualitative deterioration in the extent to which many providers of service are truly interested in the well-being of their customers, take time with them, respond to them, and are sympathetic to them.

The changes in the experience of the average patient, whether in the Medicare program or in private insurance, over the last ten years, conveys a mixed message at worst. While the distance between the average Medicare, Medicaid, or privately insured patient and the uninsured patient is infinitely larger, our ability to take care of people with technological resources continues to increase.

So this is the challenge we face. I think there is what, in Washington, we like to call a win-win solution. But it is hard to find, hard to keep your eyes on, and very hard to manage organizations to get you there. It seems that the only way to avoid falling into difficult traps is to try to keep your focus and commitment on a clear sense of who your customer, or patient, is. We need to focus on what that customer or patient not only needs, but wants, over time. Corporations, health care organizations, and government organizations that have most systematically thought about this and have most systematically listened, have done the best and are most likely to thrive.

It is inevitable that the majority of efforts to reorganize and restructure the way we do business will fail either in terms of not improving quality or not reducing costs or, in many instances, both. If we care about the long-term well-being of our current patients, those whom we are now not serving, and those in the next generation, this is a task that must be undertaken.

PART II

Voices from the Field: The Economic Pressures on Patients and Practitioners

——————— *Introduction by Ellen D. Baer* ———————

In this section of the book a panel of courageous individuals describe their experiences in the field. They are: a former patient from California, Hilary Abramson, who is also a journalist; a nurse from Washington State, Janie Storr; a physician from Massachusetts, Jack O'Donnell; a nursing administrator from Maine, Eloise Balasco; and a hospital administrator from Massachusetts, John O'Brien.

They are courageous because many people in the health care field today are experiencing economic blackmail if they dare to speak out about the risks to patients that are taken by institutions seeking to increase profits. In response to our Op-Ed articles (1994, 1995) Suzanne Gordon and I have been contacted by people from all over the country who have experienced realignments in their positions, reductions in their fees, and even job losses if they are suspected of whistle-blowing about the enormous risks to patients in the current health care situation. One nurse from a Northeastern state lost her job because she posted one of our articles on her hospital unit bulletin board.

Americans are used to the right of free speech, but many don't realize that, as employees, those protections change. Employees are considered to have a duty of loyalty to their employer that can be used to curtail free speech. Employees may be at risk if they are not protected by an employment contract, union or some sort of other association. While many states have protections for whistle-blowers, the level of protection changes from state to state, and people have to find out what protection applies to them in their state. For the most part, one is better off as part of a group, and I'm not necessarily talking about a union. Any group is protective, such as a group of nurses to advance patient care. Any kind of a group offers more protection than an individual who speaks out in a casual or independent way.

The following stories come from a wide geographic and professional interest spectrum. This broad sampling enhances the collective nature of the testimony and dramatically demonstrates our finding that the health care refocus from patients to profits is an issue affecting all parts of the country and all groups of health care providers. This is a national phenomenon that exposes patients to risks that are increasing daily, such as misidentified surgical sites, erroneous medication dosages, unattended patients bleeding and in pain, newborn infants dying of simple problems easily managed if detected early, and on and on.

I believe that what we are witnessing reflects a growing sense across this country that there is something just not quite American about being dependent. Too many political speeches, corporate papers, television ads, and media extravaganzas give the impression that people who are very old, very young, sick, or needy in some way are just not pulling their weight. Somehow, it seems, red-blooded Americans ought to be able to care for themselves no matter what their age or health status.

I am deeply concerned that the so-called corporate health movement is causing our most dependent and vulnerable neighbors to rely on, as their first line of care provider, unskilled persons who have very little knowledge, few options, and no power to effect anything on behalf of themselves, let alone the people for whom they are now being made responsible. People who assist professional staff have a long, honorable, and necessary place in health care, but they should not be on the front lines of clinical care, nor should they be performing intrusive procedures on patients.

Further, I am thoroughly puzzled by a society in which people claim that their family members are their most cherished life partners, but who opt to support a system which allows those same family members to be cared for in this terribly risky manner. What they seem unable to comprehend is that if all the expert clinicians are laid off, except for the few who will ''supervise,'' there will be no expert clinicians left in the system to provide the expert care when their highly valued family members need it.

Those of us whose business it is to care for dependent people know these things and hope to use our outrage as fuel to energize the discussion and move us to broad solutions.

As is appropriate for a book on this topic, our first chapter is by a patient, because that's the whole point: Patients must come first.

CHAPTER 2

A Patient's View

Hilary S. Abramson

For 24 years, you're identified as a journalist. Then one day, you're a professional ex-patient. I can just hear my mother, "A professional ex-patient? This is a career?" It is precisely because I was trained to observe that when I applied my hospital experience to the thousands of potential patients in the United States, I felt compelled to get the story out.

During 1994, I entered the California Pacific Medical Center in San Francisco for an unexpected hysterectomy. I had read that it was merging with Children's Hospital, but what did that have to do with me? It was known as the best hospital in the city, top of the line, state of the art.

During the preceding 5 years, I had undergone eight surgeries in three different hospitals. Excepting a blown-out left knee from a skiing accident, the surgeries related to my eyes and culminated in an 8-hour procedure on the right retina that failed. So I know something about hospitals. And this one had been the site of that last heroic effort and the one before, which put me in a positive mood about having to go back.

As a patient, you focus on the procedure and the surgeon, not the facility. This was the place where nurses had hovered over me, held my hand, explained what I would see from the world of pumped-up, artificial, vitreous fluids. This was the hospital where a favorite nurse walked into the operating room with me, hugged me, and talked me through anesthesia nausea. This was where, when I rang for help, it came; where they anticipated my needs, loading me with blankets when my temperature told them what my mouth could not. This was where they talked me through panic attacks.

When I registered, hours before the afternoon surgery, they were, as expected, most interested in my insurance, which is a thing of beauty. I can choose any physician I want and they will cover more than half of it. They failed to mention that the hospital had averaged half a million dollars in losses a week in 1994, and had laid off about half its 4,300-person staff since 1991—many of them nurses. In welcoming me back, they failed to say that I would be lucky to find a registered nurse.

So it probably made perfect sense that the first words I remember spoken after surgery were, "Didn't you notice your I.V. needs changing?" Like Robert DeNiro in "Taxi Driver," I mentally replied, "Are you talking to me?" "Are you talking to me?"

The morphine was wearing off and I didn't know if I was dead or alive, and here was this silhouette in the door with the edgy voice, "Didn't you know your I.V. needs changing?" I was speechless. He spoke for both of us in a snitty tirade. Didn't I realize we were a team? Hadn't I received some sort of patient orientation? Why wasn't I watching my I.V.? At that moment, I realized something was wrong. I managed to ask who he was. He was not a nurse. He was an aide of some sort.

In the olden days, a hysterectomy would keep you in the hospital 5 days. Today, it's 3 days; and when you get home, you need someone to slide your legs over the edge of the bed and grab both hands and pull you onto your feet. You scream like a banshee during this process, but what the heck, you're saving your insurance company money and the hospital the trouble of housing you.

As with much surgery, doctors like to get you out of bed the day after a hysterectomy, a challenging order in my situation considering that it took most of the first day to find somebody to help me. The first morning after surgery began with my ringing for a nurse. I was lying in blood and was scared. The morphine didn't seem to work anymore and I felt the reality of being sliced and stitched. The person who responded to my ring was a 24-year-old first-year nursing student. "Was I passing the normal amount of blood?'' ''I don't know,'' she said, ''I think so.'' ''When would the pain stop escalating?'' ''I don't know. I think soon.'' She had never cared for someone after a hysterectomy and knew nothing about the operation. I asked her to find answers and, even better, locate a nurse.

After insisting I see a nurse, one finally arrived. Agitated, the nurse said my doctor should have warned me about how tough it was going to be. ''There's something wrong here,'' I said. ''I am the patient. You are the nurse. I have this feeling that you expect me to make you feel better.''

She apologized, sat on the edge of the bed and began to cry. True. She'd been working double shifts because they were so short-staffed. She feared being laid off. Her brother was dying of AIDS and she had stress overload.

Eventually, the bed got changed, my catheter removed, and meals served; but the day was almost over and I had not been out of bed. I called for a nurse. Trying to move told me that this was going to require someone strong, but the only person available was the nursing student, shorter and thinner than I.

Together, we figured how to pry my fingers from hanging onto the edge of the bed sheet, stand up without screaming, and shuffle down the corridor with the I.V. tree. I counted three nurses for about 20 patients on this postsurgical floor. Every time I cried out in pain, the student nurse cringed. I apologized. I prayed I would heal overnight. The only time I could find somebody to take me to the bathroom was at night. Otherwise, rather than wet the bed, I crawled out and into the bathroom.

Everything seemed to get done at night, when most patients were sleeping. There was one wonderful nurse who reminded me of the nurses I'd met on previous tours, full of energy, humor, and information. She also confided in me how frightened the few remaining nurses were of losing their jobs. The days were longer than the nights. As the pain medication was decreased and I experienced more pain, I needed help working the hospital bed. Ringing for a nurse brought an aide who spoke little English and exacerbated the situation.

My neck hurt from the surgical tube that had been inserted in my throat. I thought sitting up with another pillow might help. I asked the aide for a pillow. Instead, he took my pillow, lowered the mattress and forced my head back onto the mattress, which produced an intense episode of pain. Every time I rang for a nurse, he arrived. Eventually, I refused to allow him to touch me.

At one point, it occurred to me, I could call 911. But who knew if the phone was connected to AT&T, MCI, or Sprint? And do you dial 8 or 9 for an outside line? I kept envisioning a Peter Sellers movie, with me yelling into the phone, "Help, get me to a hospital." Oh, I'm in a hospital and I'm paying a thousand dollars a day. Gee, if it cost this much to be tormented and ignored after a hysterectomy, I wonder what they charge to be treated likewise after brain surgery?

After the first day, I had a roommate for about a day. She was elderly and clearly alone. I never knew what was wrong with her, but she moaned and cried, and when I realized she was not able to press the call button, I assumed the role of button-pusher, one for her, one for me, one for her, one for me. I wonder if they put her with me because they'd at least have a live body able to call for help if she took a turn for the worse.

I saw my doctor briefly every morning. In the past, one word from your doctor and everyone in the hospital shaped up. I told him what was going on and he shuddered and apologized, shook his head and said, "We're going through a transition here. I apologize. It's going to take patients like you speaking up to change anything, I'm afraid."

I'll always remember the last day of my hospital stay. I realized I was not ready to go home. I had to pry myself off the bed, since the incision had become infected in one corner and pulled and burned. Each perpendicular movement felt as if someone were plunging a knife into my body. I phoned my husband and told him to come and get me. I shuffled out to the desk and told them I was leaving. Somehow they managed to come up with the requisite paperwork. They appeared relieved to have one less person to be responsible for. Their rules required that I leave in a wheelchair, but none arrived. I never said goodbye. No one ever said goodbye to me. I left on my husband's arm and no one noticed.

What a difference from the former stays when nurses and I hugged, kissed, waved and, in the last instance, cried goodbye. A week after I got home, I wrote to the CEO of that nonprofit hospital. I told him that in his facility, the patient can know as much, perhaps more, as the caregiver; that the few nurses left were too overworked to take care of patients; that aides could not necessarily do routine tasks well and, in my case, made dangerous situations and decisions that made me feel unsafe and frightened. He never responded.

A few weeks later, he had the head nurse call. By then, I had received a computer-driven, fund-raising letter, asking me for a donation so that this outstanding medical facility could stay open. Months passed and I remained infuriated that hospitals such as this one feel so pressured to cut vital services, particularly, I'm told, because CEOs at top HMOs are making a million or more dollars a year in salaries. I wrote an Op-Ed piece about my experience. The new administrator of the hospital called me. The CEO had been moved to a new and different position and the newspaper reported that he was keeping his $300,000 a year. The administrator figured, "It's too late for us to help you, huh?," but invited me to a show and tell about how they're going to make this the hospital it used to be without having to rehire nurses. I told him he owed me nothing at this point, but he'd better roll up his sleeves, take off his jacket, walk around, and hold the hands of patients who are probably lying in their beds terrified.

I've discovered stories more surreal than mine. A friend's 5-year-old daughter, Laura, was recently in Children's Hospital in Oakland, California for pneumonia. The child was actually asked to watch her I.V. and to push the buzzer for a nurse when it got to a specified level in the bag. I have also read that there actually are patients who have made 911 calls from their hospital beds when no one came when they pushed their call buttons.

Still, what I have come to call "hospital-speak" continues to build a language. Aides are often called care associates, and the patient has become a consumer. Well, I can tell you that when you're lying there trying to remember what feeling good feels like, you are not a consumer. You are not shopping. You are spending, mostly expending, more energy than you have on things that you should not have to worry about. The crisis that brought you to this hospital is all that should be on your mind, not being safe, or clean, or ignored.

I'm amazed that this kind of story is not what everybody is talking about at the coffee latte machine, at restaurants, or while commuting. I have to believe that most Americans have neither been hospitalized recently in one of these facilities, majoring in what they're calling deskilling, nor have had loved ones in these places. I am convinced that, unless something changes, this has to become the main topic of conversation in America. This will be what real people are talking about. At that point, I trust they will have arrived where I am.

Now is the time for common sense. When you go to the hospital, you have a right to expect a nurse. A person given a crash course in patient care cannot look at me and tell how I feel when I cannot speak. A good nurse can.

When I go to a hospital, I expect a nurse. If things continue the way they're going, I envision a hospital as a place where the rich bring their own nurses, and the rest of us will be lucky to share one, the way I did.

Will sick people either have to watchdog their own health care or die? We used to think of such places as other-century warehouses for the poor. With the best insurance money can buy, I felt that way little more than a year ago. When people ask me if I'm afraid to go back to the hospital, I kid and say that I don't plan to ever go back to a hospital, just as the perpetrators of this new nonhealth care craze in America must think that they will never lose their health. But the truth, of course, is that I may have to be in a hospital again. My fear is reflected in the following story: A friend of mine teaches nurses about public policy health issues. During a recent class, she asked her students to act out their fears and feelings. One nurse painted this picture: I am rushing down a hallway. There are few of us to help everyone who needs it. I pass a room with two women, one lying still and the other feebly waving at me and calling out, "She's dead. She's dead. She's dead."

CHAPTER 3

A Nurse's View

Janie Storr

I am a nurse and I work in Seattle. I work in orthopedics and neurology. I have 4 years of college experience, and I have more than 6 years of hospital nursing experience. I represent the acute care nurses who truly are witnessing firsthand the abandonment of the patients in the hospital.

Let me describe to you what I encountered when I came to work recently for the evening shift. I took report from a day shift nurse going off duty, a brief report, about her caseload. That day she had been in charge of the care of the following patients:

One 74-year-old woman with a fractured arm who had been found on the floor by neighbors the night before. She was an alcoholic woman, showing early signs of withdrawal. She had an I.V. She was alert, but not oriented, and she was to go to surgery the following day.

Another woman, 83 years old, with back pain from compression fractures in her spine, also was not oriented. She was incontinent of urine, unable to move her bowels, had a history of Alzheimer's disease, and was restrained.

Another patient, a 93-year-old woman, had had a pacemaker replaced and had been admitted to our floor because there wasn't a more appropriate

31

place to put her at that point. She was restrained and her son, I believe, had just called the hospital very concerned that her level of orientation had changed.

The fourth patient in this caseload was an 84-year-old woman who had her leg amputated at the pelvis, subsequently had a stroke, and had complete paralysis on one side of her body. She was alert, but unable to speak. She had a tube-feeding. She had blood pressures running in the 200s systolic, that were being treated with medication that had to be ingested through the feeding tube.

The next patient, a 92-year-old man, had had a craniotomy, had been transferred to a rehab unit, where he had had a stroke for which he was returned to our unit. He was currently alert, but not able to speak, had a tube-feeding, had an I.V. and catheter, had skin breakdown on both hips and also on the sacrum, and had just been diagnosed with pneumonia.

The next patient was a 75-year-old who had had a repair of a total hip fracture. This patient was a retired pharmacist who was taking multiple medications. He had a history of substance abuse and had multiple psychosocial problems, including depression. He was also a diabetic. He was discharged in the middle of the shift to another unit.

The last patient in her case-load was a 37-year-old man who had herniated a disc and come for surgery. He had a history of multiple narcotic uses and multiple back surgeries. He was currently in pain and he was crying. He was threatening to leave the hospital against medical advice, but he was unable to walk and he had been unable to urinate for 10 hours.

This is the case-load that one nurse was responsible for during the day shift at my hospital. Now, that is just an incredible caseload, in my opinion. I can't even fathom doing everything that needs to be done for all of those patients in an eight-hour period of time.

I said to the nurse, "It sounds like you had a rough day" and she said, "Well, the good news is, it was a Sunday and when I discharged a patient, I didn't get another admission."

Five years ago, nurses would comment about a heavy patient case-load, trying to ensure that one particular nurse wasn't carrying more than one patient who required a particularly heavy amount of work. Today, all the patients are heavy. They have multiple problems or they would be in the community, being cared for in a home-care situation. These patients require intensive care, but they are placed on regular hospital care floors, and assigned in groups of seven, eight, nine, or ten to a single nurse.

Night nurses on my unit commonly carry nine patients. The decreased length of stay in a hospital means that anyone even remotely able to leave is discharged. Therefore, whoever is left in the hospital is, by definition, a member of an extremely sick population. Let me give you an example of a patient considered able to be discharged from my unit to home.

A few weeks ago, a 75-year-old patient returned to the hospital because he had developed an infection in a spinal wound where he had had spinal surgery. On his return, surgery was done to debride the wound and it was left open to heal naturally from the inside out. The nurse who changed his dressing in the hospital said that the vertebrae of his spine were visible, so she packed the dressing with multiple bandages many times daily, using extremely careful sterile technique. This patient was sent home with a nurse arranged to come in once a day, and his daughter was taught to change his dressing in the home. So a 75-year-old with an open spinal wound who, three days earlier, had been deemed by the physical therapist to be unsafe on his feet, was sent home in the care of his daughter, who had, as far as I know, no medical experience.

Let me tell you what happens on our floor when we receive case-loads that we don't think we can handle safely. A few months ago I was in charge on my unit when a nurse approached me. He said, "I've just gotten a call from the recovery room. They are sending me a patient who's had spinal surgery. She's lost over 1,300 cc's of blood." That's an enormous blood loss, in my estimation, for this type of surgery. It's a dangerous blood loss, and it needs to be attended to with transfusion. In fact, a transfusion had been ordered, but the blood bank could not supply the blood at that time. It was a very risky situation that the nurse didn't feel he could manage, with his existing caseload. I called the nurse in the recovery area, explained that we were staffed as we were, and that we didn't think we could safely care for the patient. She said, "I'm sorry. It's ten minutes before 9:00 PM, and the recovery room closes at 9 o'clock." So, as you can see, business decisions are taking priority over medical decisions in the hospital!

However, I subsequently talked to the nursing supervisor. There were no ICU beds available, but we did get authority to have the nurse come from the recovery room to care for the patient on our floor. This arrangement required much assertiveness on my part. I don't think that this has ever been done before in my hospital, to my knowledge.

Technically, theoretically, a nurse is supposed to accomplish the following things for every patient on every shift: Nurses initially take a health and medical history, and we know the current complaint. We interpret doctors' orders. We provide for patient safety. We know all medications prescribed, their interactions and whether they're appropriate for the patient. We administer medications. We regulate I.V. fluids and give I.V. medications. We give blood transfusions. We treat pain. We modify pain treatment if necessary. We follow lab results and report significant values to physicians. We evaluate mental and physical limitations. We develop a care plan that is appropriate for each patient. We evaluate patients for nosocomial illnesses. We evaluate diet, appropriateness of diet, and the patient's tolerance of diet. We evaluate the patient's ability to swallow and to ambulate. We provide safe, dignified means of toileting. We evaluate wounds. We evaluate for skin breakdown. We're alert to signs and symptoms of infection. We protect privacy and confidentiality, and we support and teach family and patients. We identify psychosocial needs. We evaluate patients' lung, kidney, and heart function on an ongoing basis. We're alert to allergies. We regulate blood sugars, and we're constantly monitoring a patient's condition. We're responsible to report significant changes to a physician. Nurses are the eyes and ears of the physician when he or she is not in the patient's room.

Can you imagine doing all of this, simultaneously, for the seven patients I described earlier? How can we possibly do this? Nurses all over the country are stressed and are aware that we are not able to do what is being asked of us currently, but advocacy is not easy. I can speak from personal experience. I've been interviewed on local radio in the Seattle area. With other nurses I spoke to the King County Council, as arranged through the nursing union. And the nursing union subsequently asked me to speak to the Washington State Senate about the current situation in hospitals and the staffing situation for nurses. Subsequently, I was called into work an hour early by upper-level management. I was interrogated. I was intimidated. I was asked questions that I believe were leading me into the breach of patient confidentiality. I believe the intent of the meeting was to fire me. Only through the support of 30 other union nurses who came to the meeting on one-hour notice, do I believe I still have a job.

Nurses are exhausted. They're frustrated and they are demeaned by this current situation. We leave the hospital wanting to forget our jobs. Some nurses think it's their fault. They think if they were better organized, that they could accomplish these situations. Union activity is the only means I have found to improve hospital situations. It's the only way I've seen any success in fighting these staffing changes.

Four or five years ago, nurses in my hospital were told that nurses' aides would be hired to assist us with care. We were relieved. We needed help bathing and dressing patients, changing their beds, taking their blood pressures and temperatures, getting supplies to the unit, getting specimens to the labs, and other such tasks. We welcomed these very valuable additions to our staff. But in the current situation of poor nurse staffing, nurses' aides are likely to work beyond their level of ability in an attempt to fill in for overworked nurses, and that is scary.

For example, I worked one day with the assistance of a certified nursing aide (CNA), who had 40 hours of training and then came to the unit to work. I asked him to take blood sugars on a number of our patients. He checked back with me, in passing, a few hours after checking the blood sugars and said to me, "Oh, I forgot to mention this to you, but I didn't think it was that important. The blood sugar in room such and such is relatively low, but that's okay because the patient is sleeping." Not recognizing the coma of insulin shock, this nurses' aide, under these circumstances, was doing his best to relay to me the knowledge he felt I needed to do my job. But he was not in a position to make those kind of judgments, because he didn't have the education to correlate patient signs with disease symptoms.

In another example, I had a patient in my care who had been in the hospital for 48 hours after overdosing on aspirin. He was an impulsive individual who had had a head injury and he had stated in the emergency room that he wanted to die. When he came under my care 48 hours later, I was missing a medication that he was due. I asked him, "Do you usually take Zantac at this time of the evening?" He said, "Oh, yes. In fact, I have some in that drawer." So I opened the drawer and found more than ten vials of prescription medications next to his bedside, over 300 Tylenol in an open bottle, sedatives, tranquilizers, and psychotropic medications. This patient, at high risk to harm himself, was delivered to the unit by a nurses' aide, and these medications were placed in his bedside drawer. You wonder how that could happen. Well, how that happens is that nurses' aides are not trained to make judgments about what's safe for a patient to have. Nurses' aides are very valuable assistants to nurses, but they, too, are being abandoned at the bedside because nurses are too busy to offer them adequate support.

Nurses at my hospital organized a patient care survey through the nurses' union. We did not get any information we had requested from administrators about patients' satisfaction with their care. While over 70 nurses were handing out these surveys in their off-duty hours, they were intimidated by security personnel. They took our names, demanding we wear our nametags even though we were off duty, and we were photographed from behind cars and railings in the parking garage. I thought the National Enquirer had come to Providence Hospital. We did get, however, 120 responses from patients. Many people took this opportunity to write us letters, because they had written to administrators and they hadn't gotten any response, and they knew that we cared how they felt about their stay. Patients were not satisfied with their care on the general hospital acute care floors. The surveys indicated that nurses appeared to be under a lot of pressure; that the nurses didn't have enough time to give patients needed attention; and that it frequently took longer than 5 minutes for a nurse to come when patients called for a nurse. They were satisfied with care in units that had high nurse-to-patient ratios, like the ICU, labor and delivery, and the outpatient surgery areas.

Let me highlight a response that we got from one person who returned a survey. This letter was sent to a Providence Hospital administrator about a woman's husband's stay when he had had a series of strokes and, subsequently, I believe, died within the year, from his condition. She described finding her husband restrained to a wheelchair at the arms, but his bottom had slipped down off of the chair and he was thrashing, trying to get his bottom back up on the seat. She went for help, but no nurse was at the nurses' station, so she asked two people in the hallway to help him up into the chair. "Why," she asked, "are they so short of nurses?" Later, she detected a deterioration in her husband's condition. She believed that a physician or a nurse should have detected this deterioration. "Where," she asks, "have all the nurses gone from the hospital?"

In conclusion, the only reason that I think the hospitals are surviving at all is because nurses are so smart and so dedicated and have a sixth sense about what people need. We are the glue holding this broken system together, but we're running out of steam. And I think that putting nurses back at the bedside is the only answer to returning safe and dignified health care to America's hospitals.

CHAPTER 4

A Physician's View

John M. O'Donnell

would like to preface this chapter by openly admitting that I am
not an economist, I'm not an accountant, and I'm not a business
administrator. I am, however, a clinician, a practitioner, and I'm a
physician. I've taken care of patients every day and, with this in mind,
there are three issues that I'd like to address.

The first is that of nursing cutbacks in health care reform. I am an
intensivist, which means that I work almost exclusively in acute care
units, where nurses assume a considerable amount of responsibility for
the sickest patients in the hospital. They're expected to employ sound
clinical judgment when evaluating organ system function and administering sedatives, narcotics, and muscle relaxants.

Being at the bedside places nurses in an ideal position to reevaluate a
patient's overall condition and recognize subtle changes in vital signs,
mental status, and cardiopulmonary parameters that may herald the onset
of organ system deterioration. Nurses also contribute another vital, yet
often unrecognized and unappreciated element of acute care. They function
as a central processing unit for all the communication between physicians,
patients, paramedical personnel, and patients' families.

Despite the importance of high nursing-skill levels in the care of the critically ill patients, many institutions are downscaling the nursing labor force, resulting in decreases in nurse-patient ratios. In addition, in an ongoing attempt to save money, hospitals will take any avenue possible to avoid paying overtime wages. This has resulted in a substitution of pool, float, and agency nurses for full-time critical care nurses.

Until recently, a patient with multiple organ failure, clearly the sickest patient in the hospital, would be cared for by two nurses working 12-hour shifts, both fully familiar with the patient's problems, progress, and decision-making process. This is now the exception. Instead, four, five, or even six nurses may be responsible for that same patient over a 24-hour period. Institutional budgeting and nursing decline has all but erased primary nursing and continuity of care from the patient care plan. Institutions argue that a critical care nurse is a critical care nurse and have initiated what has come to be called cross-training.

In cross-training, a single nurse is trained in more than one specialty area and then is considered capable of working in any critical care setting. A coronary care nurse may be sent to a surgical recovery room. An emergency room nurse might have to work a night shift in a medical intensive care unit, and so on. Well, the concept of cross-training started with athletic footwear. In my opinion, that's where it should stay.

The concept implies mediocrity. Cross-training is for dabblers; it's for amateurs, and it should not be applied to sick patients. If you're a serious long-distance runner, you buy a running shoe. If you're a collegiate basketball player, you buy a basketball shoe, and if you really want to win at tennis, you buy the best tennis shoe that you can afford. I want the best-trained nurses taking care of my family and my patients. I don't want fill-ins. I don't want substitutes—and America shouldn't either.

The second issue that I'd like to address centers around the fundamental restructuring of our health care. There is no question in my mind that large amounts of money are wasted in our current health care system, and that change is necessary. This change cannot come from private-interest groups and for-profit organizations. It can't come from a system where the provision of less care is economically rewarded. It has to come from government initiatives that direct budgetary efforts toward the elimination of administrative and clinical waste, frivolous malpractice litigation, inflated pharmaceutical and equipment cost, and physician spending.

In today's hospitals, all over the country, concern for controlling cost is creating an atmosphere that is compromising quality patient care. Let me give just a few examples: In many hospitals, physicians are being discouraged from using epidural analgesia, an extremely effective method of controlling postoperative pain. Why? Because it prolongs the length of hospital stays, resulting in greater expense to the hospital and the insurer. As a result of this present health care reform, acute and chronic pain control has been placed in the shadow of medical economics.

Or consider the phenomenon of early discharge. A 70-year-old woman with chronic renal failure undergoes right forearm surgery in order to establish vascular access for hemodialysis. She is discharged home the same day, despite the fact that she lives alone, with no ancillary help available. That same night, as she's climbing the stairs in her home, she loses her balance. Being unable to grab the railing with her right hand, she reaches across her body with the left, causing her to fall backwards, down the steps, fracturing her right hip. This scenario has become all too common.

The third and final issue is that of data. Medical officials continue to dispute the claims of deteriorating patient care, demanding scientific evidence. Yet, they, themselves, have little data supporting their own position. If a town council decides to replace a traffic light with stop signs, those same individuals are obligated to monitor the number of accidents that occur as a result of that decision. Many work-redesign schemes have been implemented without ever having been tested. Hospital and managed care bureaucrats initiated these changes. The burden of proof lies with them, not with the nurses and physicians. "Outcome" has become a popular term used when referring to the scaling down of medical resources and staff. But mortality and readmission rates should not be the only measures of quality. The entire ambulatory, hospital, and discharge experience, including what patients and families experience at home, needs to be judged critically.

We, as physicians, nurses, and health care professionals, must generate the courage to challenge governmental, organizational, and institutional decisions that we feel have a negative impact on patient care. We are obligated to retain the integrity of the entire health care team, particularly during this period of financial uncertainty. We must align and crusade not only to re-establish the fundamental goals of health care, but to assure our patients' overall well-being. The health care policy makers, corporate executives, and hospital administrators who have little understanding of the urgent realities of illness should not be permitted to govern our health care system. Instead, it is the primary health care providers and their patients who should drive the decision-making process that will lead us into the next century.

CHAPTER 5

A Nursing
Administrator's View

Eloise Balasco

The preceding chapters provide persuasive evidence that the political and economic pressures on patients and practitioners are real, as health care is increasingly understood and lived as a business. I would like to address those pressures from the perspective of a nurse executive, a position which I have held for the past seven and a half years in an acute care community hospital in Portland, Maine.

My perspective comes out of balancing the tension between the responsibilities of hospital executive and those of the leader of a major clinical discipline. In my position, I am accountable for the management of the largest number of hospital employees and the largest hospital budget and, therefore, carry a profound fiduciary responsibility made more acute by rising costs and diminishing revenue streams. As the chief of the clinical discipline of nursing in my organization, I am accountable for ensuring that all patients receive nursing care that is of excellent quality and highly effective, and that the practice setting is conducive to the refinement and strengthening of that clinical discipline.

To be successful, I must be effective as both an organizational leader and a professional leader. For me to be one without the other puts both at risk. In recent years, there has been an increased emphasis on the word "executive" in the term "nurse executive" at the expense, I believe, of preserving and extending the practice of nursing. The seduction of the corporate role has blinded some nurse executives to the understanding that the real power in this position comes from proximity to the patient, the person around whom the organization's work purports to center.

Today, many practicing nurses question the values driving organizational decisions that have an impact on their ability to carry out their work with patients and families effectively. At a time when leadership is most needed, some nurses feel abandoned by their leaders. The economic pressures discussed in earlier chapters have led most hospitals in this country to experiment with work redesign in order to increase efficiency and productivity. Because patient care is the central component of the hospital's work and most patient care is given by nurses, much attention has been focused on the work of the nurse. However, unless the work that nurses do with patients and families is correctly understood, decisions could be made which threaten the quality of patient care and which, over time, have a negative impact on the hospital's ability to carry out its core mission.

I came to understand the work-redesign paradigm through an experience with a national consulting group whom we had engaged to assist us in assessing operational efficiency at our hospital. The work-redesign paradigm is based on the assumption that providing nursing care is about doing tasks and procedures in an expeditious manner and that these tasks can be rank-ordered from highest to lowest skill. The tasks requiring the highest skill are reserved for the nurse, while all other routinized low-risk nursing tasks are absolutely delegated to less-skilled or multiskilled workers. It's interesting that we have chosen to equate the terms less skilled and multiskilled. The nurse then supervises these workers and delegates to them, only interacting with a patient to assist, teach, and perform other activities requiring higher level nursing skill. Since the routine activities of patient care are now in the hands of assistive personnel, the conclusion of the work-redesign paradigm is that fewer nurses are needed to perform the supervisory and delegatory functions. Hence, significant dollars can be saved.

What I have come to know, after being a nurse for many years, is that only within a sufficient and continuous trust relationship between the patient and me, that special human relationship that binds one who is ill to one who professes to help, can I know what matters to this patient and, therefore, what can be discounted and what is the most effective way to promote healing for this particular person. I learned long ago that two different people with the same medical diagnosis most often respond in very different ways to being ill and that my effectiveness as a nurse is highly dependent on my recognizing and understanding those differences. I learned long ago that giving the bath is often about more than giving the bath. What is badly misunderstood in the work-redesign paradigm is that if the nurse and the patient cannot have a sufficient and continuous relationship, there can be no care.

We decided, after careful deliberation, to reject the recommendations by the consultants that would fundamentally change the way persons coming to our hospital for care perceive their experience. We believe that our competitive edge will continue to be the fact that when people select our hospital, it is because they feel that who they are as individuals is understood, respected and responded to. This does not mean that we are not changing things. Indeed, we are, to the consternation of many nurses on our staff, but our overarching goal is to keep the nurse and the patient together in the practical activities of care.

The ancient grounding of the practices of medicine and nursing in care and compassion is now challenged by an economic paradigm that defines those practices as things to do for a particular disease that are measurably effective (Pellegrino, 1985). Tasks and procedures can be counted from a distance, but human caring, highly skilled practical knowledge and expert clinical judgment acquired over time by nurses genuinely engaged in practice can never be understood from a distance.

These essential qualities of expert nursing practice allow the nurse to implement the instantaneous therapies which often make the difference between good outcome and deleterious consequence, and to perform these therapies in a way which respects the distinct needs and human concerns of the individual entrusted to the nurse's care. We do not have good public language to talk about the knowledge and skill embedded in caring practices, and so our tendency is to measure what the nurse does rather than whether the patient's needs are met. Tasks and procedures are then misconstrued for practice. While there is a place in care-delivery models for persons who assist the nurse, assistive personnel cannot simply be substituted for nurses if care is to be given and received.

As nurses, we have a responsibility stemming from our roles as professionals and citizens of this country, to address the issue of health care cost and quality. The economic shift in health care is real, and no one would argue with the fact that there are efficiencies to be gained. Restructuring work is not inherently bad. Resisting change or trying to preserve the status quo will serve no one well, least of all persons who need care. But the central question is what to change.

Do we want our hospitals to become places where we go to have things done to us, or places where we go for care? In our haste to respond to the economic pressures thrust upon us, we cannot lose sight of the critical human values that give meaning to our processes of care, values that only can be lived out in the relationship between the clinician and the patient. Dismantling that relationship will put the patient at risk and will continue to erode the public's fundamental trust in all health care.

CHAPTER 6

A Hospital Administrator's View

John O'Brien

I am the CEO of a health system in Cambridge which is the second largest provider of care to the indigent in Massachusetts. We provided free care to 25,000 different individuals last year. We're also known as kind of a turnaround situation. Seven or eight years ago, we lost $10 million. But, when we all pulled together, we not only eliminated that deficit, we won the most coveted award from the American Hospital Association—the McGaw Prize—which my colleagues and I take a great deal of pride in. We're doing some wonderful things at Cambridge. We've grown. We're now a hospital center, with eight or nine subacute health centers doing some wonderful things. I've got great people to work with. Sometimes, as we struggle to survive as a public hospital, it would be very easy for all of us to become disillusioned, but we can't have that happen.

Robert Wood Johnson has a reachout program that I have participated in, and we're trying to improve access to health care for the 40-something-million uninsured Americans. We discuss many devastating issues, such as that there are now 2.7 million uninsured people in Los Angeles County alone, not including the 1.5 million undocumented aliens there, as well. One of the issues discussed is a project in L.A. County to improve health care to the 40,000 foster children in the County. It is an example of the many heroes and heroines out there working on these issues.

I have to disagree with Bruce Vladeck on a couple of things, even though I am a great admirer of his. One is relative to Medicare, which Bruce thought that we may revisit in the next generation. I think that we will revisit that in three or four years, because the system very well could break in that period of time, considering the size of the cuts and the enormous burden of illness that we have, particularly in the urban areas. Second, Bruce credits the corporate medical groups for activities that raised patient satisfaction that were actually developed by the voluntaries and the not-for-profits some time ago. They may have copied them from industry, but I think they came out of the voluntary sector.

I run a system in a town that is very progressive in its approaches to a lot of issues. We are affectionately known as the People's Republic of Cambridge. But I am also the chairman of the Massachusetts Hospital Association Board. Cambridge is a very interesting place. Woolhandler and Himmelstein are from Cambridge Hospital. Physicians for National Health Program originated at the Cambridge Hospital, and a lot of the data that they started with came from us and the head of our reimbursement division. We also showed them how the Medicare cost reports work.

But I am a contrarian, and I speak across the country relative to CEO accountability. If we're going to transform health care, we are going to have to transform its leaders, and that's not simply CEOs, because we are not going to solve the problem by taking all the CEOs out and shooting them. These are really institutional and structural problems. Institutional boards of governance must be persuaded by their community members of what the community wants. People must speak out to insist on diverse memberships for these boards so that all groups are represented in institutional governance. We cannot allow white, male bankers and corporate people to decide the health care futures for all citizens. They don't understand medicine. They understand balance sheets and income statements. The political sentiment in this country today just flies in the face of the demands that we are placing on all the people who are serving our communities.

In Cambridge, we have a wonderful public health model. It is actually killing me on the in-patient side, because we're reducing unnecessary hospitalizations and readmissions. We started a free care pharmacy because we had so many readmissions of our indigent patients. We used to fill one or two prescriptions a day, and now we do 60 or 70. Our admissions are going through the floor on this; meanwhile, the hospital's administrative costs are absolutely enormous.

If you have looked at the Boston Globe recently, in the Metro Section, you would have seen that virtually two-thirds of it was filled with full-page ads by Partners, Massachusetts General Hospital, the Brigham and Women's Hospital, and other large health systems. Those ads cost $30,000 to $40,000 apiece. In addition, there are administrative expenses such as utilization review, financial analysis, and endless numbers of other bureaucratic managers on hospital salary. Our CFO always tells me, "If you give me another financial analyst, I'll return the salary ten times over." I believe that, and that salary is competing with front-line nurses and other clinicians. It is a terrible dilemma.

A couple of years ago, we had been struggling, despite the fact that we really turned it around over the last several years. And for the second largest disproportionate care provider, we've been in the black for five years, but we had to tighten the belt and we did it the way that a lot of people do, by spreading the pain around. We had cut back on some nursing in the ICU and on our telemetry unit. We are heavily unionized and we have worked relatively effectively with our unions.

One day I walked up on the unit and a nurse walked up to me and she said, "John, I gotta talk to you." And she unloaded on me. And, you know, it might have been a little bit too much, but I got it. I spent three days working with nurses on these issues to see if there were other ways, and this nurse just walked me through a case. She said, "John, this patient is post-MI and I have not had ten minutes to spend with him on patient education, and he's going home today and I'll tell you, this is not good." She walked me through, case by case, and, in the end, we added back $200,000 the next day.

Public hospitals are the safety net, and people are going to be hurtling through it before long. Public hospitals are very endangered. There used to be more than 20 municipal hospitals in Massachusetts. Cambridge will be the last, after Boston City becomes not-for-profit. The last. We'll be the last publicly owned, publicly managed hospital. I'm a public employee.

We all have to speak out. I was with the National Association of Public Hospitals recently, and Emily Freedman delivered a wonderful, wonderful presentation about the fact that we all need to speak out. Some of our most compelling spokespersons are frontline people. But not enough people are speaking out.

We saw it over the last 3 or 4 months with AHA. I'm very disappointed in AHA because I've worked with them. We have to start holding accountable our CEOs and our boards, our state associations, all of our professional associations—to start hitting a lot harder. And we have to do something about the intimidation, too. I'll be honest with you. I met with Newt Gingrich's people and they had their fingers in my face saying, "If you hurt the two Republican Congressmen up in Massachusetts, we'll punish you people." They were threatening us with $450 billion worth of cuts. That's like kicking the carcass. We have to create some ads and go to the airwaves.

This political shift to the right that we are experiencing is due to what I call a disconnect in the Beltway about what's going on and what people are facing in the clinical areas. Two good examples of disconnect are the proposals on school lunches and our immunization money. We have improved immunization rates from 60 to 80 percent over the last year and a half, and they want to wipe out our money. That's crazy; they don't get it. And I don't think that we've made the argument yet that will convince them. The public really doesn't understand this, and the stories across the country are just heart-wrenching; at times, I want to weep. But at other times, I just want to redouble my effort.

Number one, we have to start discussing these issues. We have to reach consensus. I said to someone yesterday, "We have to reach consensus on some of these issues, such as, is health care going to be a right?" And he said, "That was decided, John. It's not going to be." Now, I can't accept that. We need to confront these things; and then once we start getting these issues on the table, we can reach a consensus. And even if it is that there is going to be some sort of rationing, I can almost deal with that if we can come to some agreement rather than everyone in Washington telling me that this is doable, and that this is in my best interest.

After we reach consensus on these issues, we have to hold one another accountable. Finally, I think we can work more effectively with the corporate world, because, clearly, business has to play an important part in this. We can bring business to the table calmly, rather than kicking and screaming, by trying to align our incentives with theirs. Then we must have boards administering these systems that are in touch with their communities. I recently spoke at a trustee meeting and there might have been 80 or 90 people there, but at least 80 of them were men, and everyone in the audience, save one, was white. This was in a diverse community. Finally, I think that CEO compensation should be tied first and foremost to the improvement of the health of the community rather than to the bottom line.

PART III

Rescuing Quality Care: Perspectives and Strategies

Introduction by Suzanne Gordon

The next section of the book will reflect on perspectives and strategies about where to go from here to rescue patients and to inject values into a system which seems driven only by cost.

A somewhat recent issue of *Modern Health Care* announced on the cover that California HMOs were moving East (Lutz & Pallarito, 1995). The article said that, in California, the large purchaser groups of employers were not interested in quality, only cost, and the HMOs could not compete in California on quality, only on cost. And so they were trying to move into other markets where that idea hadn't caught on yet. That was a sobering thought.

I am a journalist and I have been covering health care and nursing and women's issues for years. I became interested in this current situation when I started hearing worrisome things from nurses to whom I had been talking for about ten years. These nurses had been developing a feeling that there was improvement on quality, that nursing was gaining a greater voice, that there were more experiments in collaboration, and so forth.

Then, suddenly, it all started to turn around about two and a half or three years ago and then, increasingly, in the past year. I started to hear more and more terrible stories from nurses and doctors who reach out to me. And nurses do not often reach out to journalists.

When I started getting phone calls from nurses, I began believing what I heard. Some of the administrators say, "Oh, they're just complaining about their jobs," and "They're just defending their own self-interest." Believe me, if nurses were good at that, they wouldn't be where they are today. Nurses are not good at defending themselves, and have not been good at defending themselves, and should be better at defending themselves. So I tend to trust nurses when they complain, just because I know they have such difficulty doing it.

Then I started getting calls from doctors, and patients, and so forth. Let me tell you about two of the conversations I had with physicians recently. One is a very wonderful physician in Cambridge, who said to me, "You know, it's really getting to be awful with the economic incentives that insurers are putting on us." She said, "When a patient with a bilateral breast cancer comes into your office, you look at her and your heart sinks." "Why? Not because you feel so terrible because she has breast cancer, but because she's going to ruin your cost profile," and then she said, "That is pretty depressing. They're turning us into people we don't even like."

And I spoke with a physician in New Jersey who is the obstetrician who spoke in public about the OB Express Bill. When I interviewed her, she described a situation in which a major HMO representative came to her office with a chart that listed the C-section rates and the average-length-of-stay rates of physicians in its plan and she was a little dot on the chart.

The representative from the HMO said they liked her C-section rate because it was below the mean, but her length-of-stay data was above the mean. Because her C-section rate was below the mean, they were not going to deselect her. But, if she didn't get her length-of-stay data down by the next year, she was out, which, of course, meant that she wouldn't be able to practice in that area. She said to me, "I realized it was either my patients or me." And that's why she spoke out about the bill mandating 48-hour length of stay, because she could not withstand the pressure.

If we are hoping for heroes, we should not hold our breath, because most people cannot be heroes. It is distressing when people who are in the profession of caring for the sick begin to feel that the sick are a drain on their financial resources. It is a very dangerous situation.

I grew up in a medical family. My father was a very conservative doctor and I grew up during the 1950s and 1960s with the boogeyman of socialized medicine. Socialized medicine meant we would have no choice of physician or hospital. We would have large bureaucracies, detached from the patient, managing care. We would have the lowest common denominator of care given to patients. We would have no continuity of care.

And, of course, that is precisely what we have backed into today with, not big government, but big business. It is quite an interesting situation, to see us today with another large bureaucracy, the corporate one, dictating to us.

Doctors have long been criticized for failing to listen to individual patients, and for insisting that they had more knowledge about their patients' bodies than the patients who live in those bodies day in and day out. If it was bad medicine when doctors dictated to patients and disregarded their concerns, why is it suddenly good medicine when health care bureaucrats, who have never even laid eyes on the patient, do the very same thing? Can bureaucratic marketplace mechanisms that depend on the stability and predictability of the production process—because bureaucracies are supposed to make things stable and predictable—deal with the instability and unpredictability of illness?

In our search for dollars in health, have we, in fact, forgotten that the real purpose of health insurance is to protect us from the cost of illness? After all, 10 percent of the population uses 72 percent of the health care resources. Why? Because they're sick.

Why has the mass media done such a very poor job of covering the really revolutionary developments in health care, aside from occasional round-ups of horror stories? And in a country that prides itself on being a democracy, why has the arrival of corporate managed care and corporate domination of health care so often been depicted as inevitable, even by those who decry the phenomenon?

And why is a single-payor universal system said to be a pie in the sky? It is a prediction that ends up being a self-fulfilling prophecy.

In this section of the book, authors will discuss the strengths and weaknesses of managed care, and comment on the historical, legal and political implications. Clark Kerr begins the discussion with the case for managed care.

CHAPTER 7

The Case for
Managed Care

Clark E. Kerr

I share every concern discussed in this book, but I want to say that, personally, I am cautiously optimistic that the quality of health care is going to get better in this country and not worse. And I want to share some reasons why. But first, by way of background, we've discussed a lot about HMOs and managed care. And I want to give you a quick look at why employers have embraced HMOs and managed care, and why they are pushing them so hard.

There are really three reasons: Foremost is the cost issue. Managed care is simply less expensive. The California experience has been that, after all the risk adjustments for age, gender, family size, education, social/economic status, and so on, HMOs are 20 percent less expensive than fee for service.

It also has been shown that the HMO premium cost growth is going up 26 percent less rapidly than fee for service, which means that the gap is increasing. Now, why all the concern about health care costs? You've heard mostly from the nursing standpoint so far. I want to tell you a little of what happened in the business world.

I remember very clearly a meeting we had almost ten years ago in San Francisco with a group of businesses. We had a large company up from Los Angeles. They had just finished using 1985 cost data, trending their profit picture, which was going up, and trending their health care costs, which were going up even faster. Those two lines would have intersected had nothing changed—in 1995, they were going to go out of business if those trends did not change. It was a real wake-up call.

Just five years ago, *Fortune* magazine had a full-page graph that was titled, "Why Managers Should Be Scared," and it predicted that if health care costs continued at the 1990 rate, the average health care cost per employee was going to be over $15,000 annually by the year 2000. That is about half the average American salary.

At that time, I was at Bank of America, and I just extended the trend line on and estimated that somewhere around the year 2079, health care was going to approach 100 percent of GDP, which might have been fine for those of you in health care, but not so fine if you were in another business.

From 1970 to 1991, the real wages of the average American went up 0.4 percent. Over that 21-year period, wages went up less than half of 1 percent. During that same period of time, health benefits costs went up 234 times. Benefits costs went up 585 times faster than wages, and was one of the reasons that American salaries remained stagnant during that two-decade period of time.

In 1970, health costs represented 21 percent of pretax corporate profits. By 1990, health costs were 62 percent of pretax corporate profits. I remember back in the "good old days" of the 1980s, when the business community talked about UCR—remember the old "usual, customary and reasonable"—we said that what it really meant was the "usual and customary rip-off." We had a favorite saying that we used to describe our feelings about health providers: "We gave them an unlimited budget and they exceeded it."

So one reason, obviously, that HMOs and managed care became popular was simply an issue of financial survival for corporate America. But there were other reasons, too. We found out from surveys that we've been doing since 1987 in California that employee satisfaction is higher in HMOs than fee for service. And at this point in California, overall, HMOs and managed care are about 10% more popular, and rated higher, than fee for service. The national average ranges somewhere between 5 to 10% higher.

Third, employers are cognizant of the fact that about 30 percent of their costs are directly due to employees' poor health behaviors, such as smoking or not exercising, being overweight, too much alcohol, and so on. Since 1987, we have surveyed employees about how much assistance they received in the area of health counseling and health behaviors from their doctor and health plan. Consistently, from 1987 through the current time, health maintenance organizations, HMOs, have provided, on average, about twice as much health promotion counseling and lifestyle assistance as fee for service.

So basically, the conclusion that corporate America made was, if you've got more employee satisfaction, if you've got more assistance in keeping employees healthy, all at less cost, maybe there's more value in managed care and HMOs. It may be a simplistic analysis, but that was our conclusion.

Also, employers, as well as employees, liked the fact that in managed care and in HMOs, there was a tendency to treat you as a whole person. They dealt with you when you were healthy as well as when you were ill; whereas, fee for service usually only dealt with you when you were ill. And that is one of the reasons why I think HMOs are so popular in California. People want to get help staying healthy, as well as being cured when they are sick.

But the critical issue, of course, that we have been discussing today is, what happens when you fall ill, seriously ill? Is managed care really a Dr. Jekyll and Mr. Hyde? When you're not sick, the happy smile and pat on the back. When you do get seriously ill, it's the barriers, the delays, the denials, and so on? Let's first take a look at financial incentives.

We all know that the financial incentive for the fee for service is overtreatment. There are some real dangers with that, almost as many as with the reverse. I remember how stunned we were back in the mid-1980s. We looked at California data, C-sections, hysterectomies, and so on. In town after town, city after city, rural area after rural area, without exception, the hysterectomy and C-section rates correlated much more with the type of insurance that women had, than with their age or other biological factors.

If you were in fee for service, you had a 50 percent greater chance of surgery than if you were in an HMO. And California data showed that in spite of the 50 percent higher C-section surgery rate, there was no improvement in perinatal outcomes. But there was two times the cost. There was also two times the recovery time for the woman, and there was increased risk for the woman in terms of infections.

So managed care, at least in that respect was pretty good. Now, of course, everybody assumes that managed care has the financial incentive for underservice' and undertreatment. Right? Not necessarily. I want to give you some examples. We just described the example of health promotion services. Managed care organizations, the good HMOs, have understood that it can be cheaper to keep people healthy than to treat them when they're ill. And they're doing a relatively good job in that respect. The incentive is in the right direction. It's a win-win situation for everybody.

What about the issue of early detection in the treatment of cancer? United Healthcare has calculated how much it takes to treat cancer in stage three versus stage one. It costs them $132,000 more to treat a stage three breast cancer case, than if it's caught in stage one. There's a financial incentive for them to catch it early. And obviously, the outcomes are better for the woman if you can catch it in stage one.

And so what is the actual scorecard? There have been studies that have shown that when you compare HMOs (there was a study of seven states) versus fee for service if you look at who catches the most cancers in stage one, HMOs do a better job for breast cancer, cervical cancer, and melanoma (Riley et al., 1994). The incentives are in the right direction.

A third example: self-care education. It's been known that self-care can save at least 5 percent of the total cost of health care. A lot of the medical visits are unnecessary; they could have been treated at home. Not to mention that, from the employee standpoint, the consumer standpoint, there's also the issue of time inconvenience and the risk that you may sit in a doctor's office or clinic and pick up a cold from the person next to you. Kaiser and other health plans have recently given out self-care books, and different types of self-care education to their members, which fee for service has never done, because it is not an organized system of care, and it doesn't have the same incentive. Again, another case of the right incentive for managed care.

A fourth example is chronic disease management. A person who's chronically ill usually gets some sort of assistance in management from their provider. The incentive for HMOs is to do group education, because it's cheaper than one-on-one. What they found out was, when you do group education, you also create peer support which in itself generates tremendous advantages in terms of making people happier, getting them to function better, and reducing utilization of costly services. Again, an economic incentive that is positive in terms of consumers and in terms of quality of care.

This may be starting to sound like a paid advertisement for HMOs. But I want to give you one more example before we look at the flip side. I would like to look at the important issues of unevenness of care in health care and at iatrogenic disease, two critical issues.

I chair the California Health Policy and Data Advisory Commission (State of California, Office of Statewide Health, Planning, & Development) that has, for several years, been trying to evaluate quality in hospitals, not an easy thing to do, we found. We've had UCLA, Rand, UCSF Medical School, and others helping us do risk adjustments. One thing we have been able to determine—we've done the right risk adjustments, we've done validation studies, and so on—is evaluation of the treatment of MIs. And we have found—and I wouldn't be surprised if it's the same around the U.S.—that in every major city in California, between hospitals, after you've made all the risk adjustments, there are at least two-to-one differences in mortality.

A number of California HMOs now are using this data to select which hospitals they want in their network. This is a consumer safeguard that does not exist in fee for service—another positive for managed care.

"First do no harm." Let's look now at iatrogenic disease. If you believe the 1991 Harvard Medical Group study done in the state of New York, where they abstracted the thirty-some-thousand medical records and then extrapolated the results nationwide, it would appear that perhaps over 100,000 Americans die each year of preventable treatment-caused events (Leape et al., 1991). Robert Brook from UCLA once said that hospital admissions represent the number one preventable cause of death in the United States. Of course, tobacco is number one, but iatrogenic disease may be number two. It is clearly a major issue.

The adverse reactions to drugs, the hospital-acquired infections, the falls, the surgical mistakes, and so on. It's costly in lives, obviously. It's also costly in dollars. I am told the average cost to treat a hospital-acquired infection is about $2,100. The average cost to treat an adverse drug event is about $8,000. Studies have shown that most of these problems are due to systems shortcomings and systems failures as opposed to individual incompetencies.

A number of institutions, such as Brigham and Women's Hospital in Boston, have cut their adverse drug reactions (ADRs) in half simply by introducing a computerized drug-checking system. I have also read that about a third of all cervical cancer cases are missed by the traditional Pap smear exam. We know about 4,800 American women die each year of cervical cancer. There are new computerized tests that apparently can catch 92% of the cancers that Pap smears examined by the human eye miss.

There is a clear moral incentive on everybody's part—fee for service and managed care—to avoid these adverse events. But what about the financial incentive? These types of information investments cost money. From a purely financial standpoint, in traditional fee for service there is not a clear financial incentive to invest large sums of money in new computerized information systems. A longer length of stay or use of more ancillary services are charged for and usually paid, even when caused by an adverse event.

In the capitated, managed care world, the health plan or provider eats that expense, eats that $2,100 or that $8,000. There is a definite financial incentive, in addition to the moral incentive, to try to avoid these types of events. And if you look at what is happening, a number of the hospitals and the medical groups that are contracting with managed care are starting to make major investments to help avoid treatment caused injuries. Another example where managed care financial incentives can benefit the public.

One final example: fewer barriers to access to the health care system for consumers. If you're in an HMO, your financial barrier is $5 or $10 to access the system and get help. If you're in fee for service, it could be $250, $500, $750, $1,000, or whatever the deductible may happen to be. One recent California study looked at patients who had appendicitis, and found that patients who were in HMOs had 20 percent fewer ruptured appendices than those in fee for service (Braveman et al., 1994).

The study's researchers decided that probably the main reasons for the different outcomes were the minimal financial barriers to deter the HMO patients from coming in immediately as soon as they felt abdominal pain and that many of the HMOs had easy 24-hour access to a nurse or a physician.

These examples are positive in terms of managed care. But what about the people we've heard about who have acute, costly illnesses that are no longer in the preventable stage? There are several examples in this book. We've read about them in the media. I've heard five stories about HMOs this week alone, four of them negative, and one of them positive. Everybody seems to have a story. It was interesting that two of the cases were about the same HMO. And in one case, the person was planning to leave that HMO because of the inadequate service they felt they had received under a very difficult situation. In the other case, the individual couldn't say enough about how superior the coordination of care was, how excellent the specialists were, and how they saved his wife's life.

It is sometimes hard to know what the real situation is. I suspect it's somewhat of a mixed bag and most likely varies between managed care plans. Some plans are better than others. But the incentives here are obviously much more questionable. The critical issue to determine: is inappropriate, futile care being properly withheld, or is important, needed care being delayed or not being provided? Possibly both are occurring and I don't know of any easy solution to this in the near term.

But I do want to suggest three things: One is, as a temporary safeguard, we have media attention as a significant deterrent to poor quality care. No health plan, hospital, or doctor can afford negative publicity in today's competitive marketplace.

In one of the cases I mentioned earlier, a woman in Sacramento whose acutely ill aunt felt stymied by her HMO, went to the *Sacramento Bee*, which is their major newspaper, and the newspaper ran the story. The woman said as soon as the article appeared, the barriers to care went down and things happened fast. Her aunt is fine now.

But in the longer term, we have to get health care report cards, comparative performance publicly reported in these areas. That's the best safeguard and it is feasible. We need to make the market place work for consumers, and comparative information is key.

Now we have the HEDIS information that's coming out (Health Plan Employer Data and Information Set). HEDIS is nowhere close to what we are going to need, but it and other nascent efforts are important starts that need to be encouraged. The public needs to know who is doing a good job and who is not.

This requires three things:

First, we need to develop decent risk adjustment systems, so we can level the playing field and make meaningful comparisons. Not an easy job, but clearly doable if we put the resources necessary into it.

Second, we have to come up with meaningful measures that are more than just clinical indicators. We have to go to patients to find out what is important to them, in terms of functional outcomes, emotional status, and so on.

Finally, it's absolutely critical that we implement computerized patient records, so we can more readily evaluate the continuum of care and the final outcomes. We can't spend the substantial amounts of money it takes to go into chart reviews to find out who's doing a good job and who's not. When we have electronic records, we can better evaluate the entire spectrum of care. Once we have this measurement system in place, we can more accurately design financial incentives in favor of rewarding good quality care.

Some members of the business community are already beginning to work on creating a pay-per-performance system. The objective is to reward good quality of care and take away any incentives to withhold necessary care. The idea is to put some of the money that goes to health care into a performance pool; and whether a provider or health plan gets that money or not depends on how good a job they do on risk-adjusted quality of care outcomes for patients.

Consumers are going to play an increasingly important role in this area because they will begin to have information from which to differentiate between the good providers and the bad ones. If they don't choose wisely, we've lost the benefits of the new system. This requires that we start educating consumers about the information and its importance and use.

The Pacific Business Group on Health, which is the largest business health purchasing group in America, has a motto that says, "Let's go from counting quality to making quality count." The group has put 2 percent of the health plan premium at risk for meeting certain quality and satisfaction targets. They have said that you've got to meet these quality standards or else you won't get this 2 percent. It is quite an incentive to improve quality of care. The group has publicly released comparative quality scores. They are developing a statewide quality information hub for consumers that is going to give quality information at the health plan level, the medical group level, and the hospital level via telephone, fax, and the Internet. The future is going to be exciting, and if we work together and do things right, we can make health care quality significantly better than it is today.

CHAPTER 8

The Case Against Profit-Driven Managed Care

Quentin D. Young

I was at Jesse Jackson, Jr.'s celebration after he won an Illinois Congressional primary. When asked what his program was, he said, "First, to retire Speaker Gingrich." And, when asked how he felt about the Medicare and Medicaid cuts, he said, "I'm going to Congress to get a single payer Canadian system passed." So there's the first wave of your progressive vote.

I think I have to apologize, or at least warn you, that I possess a strange mixture of apocalyptic vision and mindless optimism that you might find a little confusing. The apocalypse, of course, is the horror that is being visited upon our country's health. And I'll try to convince you it is even worse than you have heard and read.

The optimism is a basic optimism that for-profit health care is generating animus which is going to be transformed into political action, that we will get thorough-going reform faster than you think—not late in the next century, not decades from now, but faster than you think. I believe that is the likelihood.

Currently, and for most of my life, I have worked in a small group of primary care internists, on a fee-for-service basis. But also, I spent ten years in the government service, at Cook County Hospital, where I was Chairman of Medicine. So you will find no enthusiast for government bureaucracy here. I also worked in a prepaid group practice in a union health center for a lot of years before I took the government job. And so I know the varieties of incentives and arrangements. And when I say that piquant phrase, "prepaid group practice," the older people will recall that's what we called those remarkable developments in the 1940s: Kaiser Permanente, Group Health Cooperative of Puget Sound, HIP, Group Health in Washington, and so on.

Those were wonderful innovations—economy of scale and group practice and emphasis on prevention—that brought health care to a lot of working people in America. They're not to be confused with today's for-profit, corporate-run HMOs. Until we get that clear, we are going to be using a jargon that makes no sense.

I've just identified the enemy. The danger in all the things we are talking about originates not from prepaid group practice. That is actually a very good way to run things at times. But it is these profit-driven, publicly held corporate arrangements that are marching to the wrong drummer. The efficient manager of those systems are charged morally, ethically, fiscally, and legally to maximize profits for the investors. A proper health care system, on the other hand, is animated, or should be animated ultimately to heighten the health status of the nation's population. Their contradictory drives put them in conflict.

We hear that our uninsured numbers are rising at the rate of a hundred thousand people per month, added to the already 40 million uninsured (Hellander, Moloo, Himmelstein, Woolhandler, & Wolfe, 1995). Now, that is the work product of the corporate system. They are the ones that are creating that reality, and they can't be exonerated from it. Our failure to do two or three obvious things has put us in this plight and when we as a nation come to understand it, we will get out of it.

First of all, we need national health insurance. I've checked Scriptures. I've checked the Constitution. It is nowhere written that the workplace is where health care must be paid for. All of these business people who are looking at rising premiums (they'd like quality too, but cost obsesses them) are being driven by an ideological rigidity that does violence to their clear-headed business sense: they must resist "government medicine."

Instead, they should let the United States join the rest of the human race, at least the Western industrial world, and recognize that health care is a right. It is a responsibility of society to assure health care. Because there's no correlation between illness and capacity to pay, except an inverse one, civilized societies must attend to that. We are in the process of abandoning our social responsibility for health care. We cannot let that happen. We need to enact a national tax-based insurance, Medicare for everybody, and end the destructive linkage of insurance with employment.

Ironically, the older not-for-profit HMOs, that is, prepaid group practices, are being caught in a vampire effect that requires them to emulate the for-profit HMOs. They, too, are being driven to speed up doctors, to cut cost, and, yes, to cherry-pick desirable patients to avoid the people who cost money, that is, sick people.

I have to rain on Clark Kerr's New Jerusalem out there in California (see Chapter 7). First I refer him to the Commonwealth Fund Report of July, 1995. It can be described as "Dissatisfaction With Managed Care In Three Large Cities." Workers enrolled in managed care plans in three major cities—Boston, Miami and Los Angeles—reported greater dissatisfaction with their health care than those enrolled in traditional fee-for-service plans. According to a Harris poll of 3,000 adults, 15 percent of managed care members rated the quality of health care services as fair or poor, compared to 6 percent of fee-for-service patients. Low-income managed care members, ominously earning less than $15,000, and workers who had no option but to join a managed care plan, captives as we know, were twice as likely to be dissatisfied, 32 percent. Managed care members were also far more likely than fee-for-service members to rate their plans as fair or poor for access to services, including specialty care, 23 versus 8 percent; emergency care, 12 versus 5 (Commonwealth Fund Press Release, 1995).

In surveying sick people—and beware surveys that don't focus on sick persons—a study was commissioned by the Robert Wood Johnson Foundation done by Harris and the Harvard School of Public Health, which can be described with the title, "Sick Persons in Managed Care Have Difficulty Getting Services." Sick persons and disabled patients in managed care plans reported more problems getting health care, 22 percent versus 13 percent, than their counterparts in fee-for-service plans, according to a telephone survey of 2,400 randomly selected nonelderly patients. Sick persons in managed care were more likely than fee-for-service patients to say they were unable to obtain needed specialist care, 21 versus 15 percent, and for diagnostic tests, roughly the same ratio (Robert Wood Johnson Foundation, 1995). This is far from a story of four or five times as good that was reported by Clark Kerr.

My concern about this system is that it's not merely bad, or that simply, some regulation will fix it. It is pernicious. It is destroying carefully crafted arrangements in this country. Patient choice is disappearing. Physician incentives are subversive. Infrastructure is being pulled out. The nursing profession is being deprofessionalized as we talk. It has been accomplished with breathtaking speed. Two years ago, there was a shortage of nurses. Today, we have all these untrained people who are displacing nurses at great patient peril. And, of course, the same kind of thing is going to happen to the medical profession next.

Certainly, I share the harsh criticism that is due physicians as a group and organized medicine in particular for the excesses, the abuses, the unnecessary surgery, the inappropriate testing, the exorbitant fees, and the flawed stewardship that opened the door to this terrible, terrible catastrophe. For awhile, in the current legislative climate, the AMA seemed to be flirting with words such as "universal care," but they have given that up. They are now instead supporting "access." For $3 billion in concessions to physicians—that was the 30 pieces of silver—the AMA has sold out to the Gingrich plan.

Unfortunately, it is familiar behavior for AMA. It opposed, bitterly and successfully, Medicare itself until 1965. Then Lyndon Johnson, trading on the national depression over Kennedy's assassination, achieved passage of the Civil Rights Act, the Voters Rights Act and, yes, Medicare, but it was a tough one. Roosevelt, with huge Congressional majorities, couldn't even get it out of committee, nor could Truman.

In the interests of full disclosure, I must confess that I am a member of the AMA. Because I live in its home city, being a member allows me, every time I see AMA leaders, to remind them that I've been a member for whatever number of years, 45 at the moment, and that I have agreed with their policies for one and a half minutes. But be assured that the disarray in the House of Medicine about their profession is significant. It's politically significant.

Doctors are having a crisis of nerve. They say such remarkable things as, that they would not choose to go into medicine again. But they say worse things than that. They say they do not want their children to go into medicine. They are dispirited and they do not know what hit them. But these are the only doctors we have, and that is an important concept, as we bash doctors. We have to win them over to taking a responsible course within the health system. To borrow from Yogi Berra, "When you come to a fork in the road, take it." There is a fork in the road. Doctors are being forced to choose, in a very fundamental way, whether they're going to ride with the hounds, which I equate with supporting the corporate takeover, or with the hares, their patients.

The only way physicians can survive as a profession, with their morality intact, their prestige intact, and their ability to care for patients intact, is if, in larger and larger numbers, they see the need for unity with the patients in these desperate times.

There has been a degradation of the medical profession, caused by market incentives, which has resulted in two-thirds of American doctors practicing as highly priced specialists. Hyperspecialization is a curse. While it is not likely that gastroenterologists will be driving taxi cabs in New York, we have, at the best estimate, 145,000 too many specialists. This disproportion was caused by paying much higher fees to "proceduralists," while diminishing the status of primary care physicians.

It does not have to be that way. We do not need the marketplace to discipline physician behavior. It doesn't discipline anyway; it discriminates. The market selectively seeks patients who are healthy; it denies care as best it can. It also moves into corruption. I refer you to an article in the *New York Times* (Feder, June 14, 1995) describing how CareMark, one of the biggest corporate providers, was fined $161 million. They agreed to the fine when they were allowed to continue their Medicare business. They could have lost their Medicare connection under the law, but since that was spared, they settled for the $161 million fine. Their stock went up. The fine, incidentally, was for kickbacks to doctors for inappropriately prescribing CareMark's home health care products. The opportunities to scam are enormous and they are learning every way.

What is the answer? The answer is to join the human race. We need a national health insurance, thank you, and we need to do it like Canada, but different, because we're richer; we have more resources; and most of the problems Canada is facing, we won't have to face. I anticipate somebody saying, "Oh, Canada is in deep trouble with their health care system. There are fiscal difficulties." There are fiscal difficulties. Canada is a poorer country than ours, with double our unemployment for example. But if Canada had our health system, Saudi Arabia would have bought it at an auction ten years ago.

We have a system that costs one trillion dollars—$3,400 per year for every person in the country. The nearest country to us is Canada with 2,200, 40 percent less. Does anybody here think we could not have a fantastic health system, taking care of everybody, taking care of the seniors, home care, long-term care, everything, at $3,400 per person?

Of course it can't happen if we have the kind of arrangement we have now where we have huge administrative waste, where we allow huge profits for these corporations from that trillion. The economics have to be mentioned. They are astounding. My favorite *Wall Street Journal* headline was in December, "HMOs pile up billions in cash, try to decide what to do with it" (Anders, December 21, 1994). English translation, "They are making so much money, they don't know what to do." But they do know what to do, buy more hospitals and doctors' practices, and buy out their competitors.

We are already approaching an oligopoly. The economist John Kenneth Galbraith has said, "Oligopolies don't compete. They share." And that is what, of course, is happening. We're getting down to six or eight big HMOs, and it has been suggested that, as in Minnesota, it will become one or two big ones. And despite all that has been said, these HMOs are, at this stage, on their good behavior. They are trying to win people and penetrate markets. If you want to see how tough they can be, wait until they control a market.

This country has a wholesome, rich mistrust of monopolies. Our legislative tradition, our national political history, is replete with successful struggle against them. While that struggle is in grave trouble now, it is my expectation that the passion for fair play in American politics is being rekindled.

CHAPTER 9

A Historical Perspective

Joan E. Lynaugh

My perspective is that of both a nurse and a historian. And I just can't help but see the events we're experiencing today in the perspective of time.

These times that we are living in seem to be both familiar and strange. This chapter deals with nursing as a historical entity and as a social institution within the context of the present.

I don't propose any solutions or strategies, but I do suggest, or perhaps just remind, that we acknowledge two things. First, there is already a lot of change in the health system. Other chapters in this book have done a good job of describing this change. Second, we have to remember that historically things do not change as much as we fear they will.

Much of our discourse on change takes place at the level of hyperbole. We shout at each other. However, in the end there is a fundamental reality that we all know about. We are humans, and like other animals, we are mortal and, therefore, we get sick and die, and we do that in a fairly predictable way. Unlike other animals, however, we almost always care for each other somehow.

In today's discourse on change in health care, we are aware that upheaval and chaos often create an opportunity for change; and, in fact, sometimes the only way you can get change is to create chaos. This is a good time to re-examine and recalculate the nature and use of our services.

For most of the twentieth century, we have had cheap nursing in hospitals. At first it wasn't paid for at all. Now we are paying for it at a rather high price. We have to consider what our systems for caring for our population will be as we all age and multiply. I will present a bit of this issue in historical context.

Professional nursing is just about a hundred years old now. It was born during one of America's earlier eras of mean-spiritedness and greed, now called the "Gilded Age." Let me remind you a little bit about the years between 1875 and 1895, roughly the last quarter of the nineteenth century. People who then called themselves Social Darwinists—and they called themselves that with pride—railed against the poor, the unproductive, the misbegotten, just as their successors do now—fearful that the failure represented by such unfortunates might reveal certain fundamental flaws in the capitalist system and bring the whole free enterprise system down.

The free enterprise system was rather new in the late nineteenth century. We had had a revolution. We had had a Civil War. We had industrialization. We had a series of severe economic depressions, but we still had faith that free enterprise could bring a better life for all of us.

The great American Dream of upward mobility and individual freedom from hereditary or class constraint was then, and still remains, a powerful source of energy and productivity. It is an idea that inspires. But it is also a myth that constitutes a base for those who argue that America cannot allow itself to be dragged down or held back by those who cannot or will not keep up.

In 1890, for example, Josephine Shaw Lowell, a Boston-bred leader of Social Darwinism, was calling for what she labeled more "scientific" approaches to giving charity to the poor. Mrs. Lowell worried that relief would be destructive of the manhood of the poor, and money expended in relief would most likely be wasted "in riotous living." At the exact same time that Josephine Shaw Lowell was making arguments against spending on the poor and dependent, in almost every small town and large town in the country, citizens were organizing to found hospitals where, in many instances, schools to train nurses would also be created.

Alice Fisher, who was a pioneer nurse reformer from Great Britain who died in 1889 in Philadelphia City Hospital, put the work of nursing in stark perspective. She said "I am sure, that of all the means by which it is possible to gain daily bread, there is none more irksome, more trying, nay more revolting, than the charge of the sick, if the nurse have not that in-borne love of the work which is given, alas, but to a few. But, on the other hand, if it so happens that she [or he] have this love in addition to other necessary mental and physical qualities, no calling can be found which offers so happy a life or where labor brings so quick and inevitable a reward or which, in spite of many undeniable anxieties, secures such absolute peace of mind'' (Fisher in Stachniewicz & Axelrod, 1978).

The parallel, but conflicting perceptions of the world, which we can see if we look at 1890, fear and distrust of the poor and the sick, side by side with altruism and faith in the potential of the human condition, comprise a somewhat unlikely foundation and circumstance for the formation of the social entity called nursing. The value of nursing to the American public then and now derives from the content of the work. Nurses care for those who either temporarily or permanently cannot care for themselves. At the level of the individual, nurses do work that others do not know how to do; that they are afraid to do; that they don't have time to do; or that they simply don't want to do.

In a more general sense, nursing's promised compassion and availability—the romantic idea of nursing—offer Americans a necessary and visible reassurance that we have constructed a civilized society, perhaps in spite of ourselves.

For five or six generations, nurses have been trusted to substitute for part of the caregiving function of the family, which is the social unit traditionally responsible for care of the very young, the sick, and the dependent. Before organized nursing existed, families hired servants to help do this work when possible and, thus, some men and women always did do nursing for pay. It was a trade handed down from parent to child.

The rise of organized nursing, however, coincides with a period in our history when we began to have, finally, sufficient income to hire people to care for us. And nursing as a distinct work became necessary because the social and economic changes of the mid- to late nineteenth century—work outside the home, geographic mobility, a rising standard of living—made continued reliance on traditional family-based care impossible, unnecessary, or at least undesirable.

Moreover, in our ambivalent way, we view care of the sick and dependent as one of the ways we try to ameliorate the harshness of our economic system. We like to think that we are a humane people. Our economic system rewards productivity and punishes failure to produce. Indeed, nursing as a distinct occupation was singled out as one part of the nineteenth century social contract Americans made with each other in the face of urbanization and industrialization. In spite of our tradition and belief in rugged individualism, we said we would act out our humane impulses. We said we would not abandon the sick and injured, our children, or the elderly; and in this sense, nursing from the beginning has reflected the changing moral and social values of Americans.

In another sense, nursing has, from the beginning, I think, been tainted by its association with these same moral and social values, which have so little to do with productivity, growth, wealth, creation, and modernity. Nursing and nurses act as the agents for Americans' prevailing view of what is right when it comes to care of the sick.

Let's take a look at the title of this book. The Random House Dictionary says that abandonment means to relinquish or leave alone, but abandonment also refers, of course, to acting heedlessly or without care for the consequences. I think Americans are more likely to act heedlessly and rue the consequences than to deliberately abandon the sick or the poor.

Silence on issues affecting the chronically ill, the elderly, and the poor, is also a kind of abandonment. The system of care we have constructed over the twentieth century relies on several interrelated balance points: First, as it's been noted earlier, it was locally derived. The hired help, the doctors and nurses and the institutions, the hospitals, were susceptible to local opinion and local control, either because they were local themselves or because their livelihood depended on favorable local opinion.

Second, the distribution of money, both public and private, through the same local systems (some of which were nonprofit and some of which were public) is used to do the work of sick care. This habit sustained our idea of local control, whether it was real or not. Medicare, now 30 years old, is only a payment mechanism. Nobody actually gets any care from Medicare.

Third, we more or less agreed that the able-bodied of the society must care for the elders and the nonable-bodied. We have vacillated over and over again in our understanding of whether that care should be the responsibility of the individual or a responsibility shared by the collective.

That seems to be the issue right now. We are back to rethinking, as we did in the nineteenth century, just how much collective responsibility we are willing to share versus how much of the burden the individual and family must assume alone and without recourse.

There's something special about the way Americans look at these issues. We do our very best to avoid the implications of our own mortality. We call it health insurance. It is, of course, sickness insurance. We hate and deny the idea that disease or accident can strike us in a random way. We always try to find a reason why it happened. And to my knowledge, there is only one hospital in the country, which happens to be the oldest hospital in the United States, the Pennsylvania Hospital, that calls its nursing organization by the most appropriate name, namely, the Department of the Sick and Injured.

We can only understand our reluctance to face the issues of paying for care by recognizing our almost traditional avoidance of the true meaning of illness and disability. Our emphasis is, indeed and appropriately, on staying well and we nurses, HMOs, and doctors say we can keep you well. It is hard for us to go into detail on just how we are going to go about doing this, since most of us also know that being and staying well is mostly a matter of genetics, age, affluence, and good luck. Just the same, the idea of staving off mortality appeals to us as optimistic Americans.

I find myself perplexed by the idea that medical and nursing care services can be dispensed in the same way that automobiles and VCRs are sold. As someone who needs and uses medical and nursing services, I just don't want to engage in an adversarial relationship as I do when I buy a car. I don't want to think that my treatment might be affected by the financial pressures bearing down on my physician or nurse. I have great confidence in the professional and moral strength of my colleagues in medicine and in nursing, but I don't want to see a system developed where their interests are pitted against mine as a patient. Their morale is badly dented by this and my trust is destroyed.

That's the nature of competition. The question is, can health care be adversarial? I don't believe it can be. We can probably agree on a few things: That the collective society should act in a civil way toward the old, the sick, the very young and the poor, not leaving it all up to them and their families; that we should act to refute the current pressures on caregivers to withhold services or refuse to treat certain sick persons; and, finally, that we try hard to stay focused on the complicated issues that are inherent in caring for the sick and not just the problem of paying for it.

CHAPTER 10

Legal Nightmares/Remedies

Ann Torregrossa

I cannot think of a time during the 15 years that I have represented consumers on health care issues when patients have been more vulnerable than they are today. And I'd like to share with you why I think they're particularly vulnerable right now.

I'm an attorney, so whenever someone comes to me and asks, "Can my HMO do this to me? Can they deny me care?", the first thing I ask to see is the contract. Your rights and your liabilities are set forth in your contract. Patient vulnerability starts with the contract, because it's not negotiated by anyone who has the patient's interests at heart. It's often negotiated, in the case of Medicaid for example, by the Department of Welfare and the HMO; in the case of the employee, by the employer and the HMO.

As Arthur Caplan discusses in his chapter, we need to begin to get those patient perspectives at the table—at the contract negotiations—so that they are represented. Often patients don't even get a copy of the contract that sets forth the health care to which they are entitled. Even if patients are entitled to health care services under the contract, they may not have the right to enforce the contract as a third party beneficiary.

Starting right from that contractual relationship for health care, patients are abandoned. Managed care has taken the only advocate that patients often relied on—their health care provider—away from them as a patient advocate. Under fee for service, patients had a wide choice of physicians. Their physician would discuss with them their treatment options. If specialist care was required, the physician would have a range of health care providers to choose from. And the physician would talk with the patient about what those choices were.

Under managed care, the patient must select a primary care physician from the limited number offered by the plan. That primary care physician has a limited number of specialists in the network from which to choose. And many of the treatment choices that were previously left to be determined through the physician–patient relationship are being controlled by the HMOs. One example is how long a new mother can stay in the hospital after she has had a baby.

Until now, we patients have depended greatly on our health care providers to be our advocates. Now, due to some really perverse financial relationships and arrangements, patients have lost, to a large extent, their physicians and other health care providers as their advocates. We know how difficult it is to find physicians and nurses who will speak out when health care is being inappropriately denied.

A case handled by the Pennsylvania Health Law Project comes to mind. I received a call from a nurse in Pennsylvania who worked for a pediatric nursing home. She was calling on behalf of a Medicaid patient who was enrolled in a Medicaid-only HMO. The 2-year-old patient had been diagnosed with a terminal condition and placed on a ventilator. The child was ready for discharge to home, which was in a public housing unit, still on the ventilator. The Medicaid-only HMO sent their home health agency out to look at the public housing unit in advance of the discharge, and refused to provide the home health care needed to bring the child home because they said it is too dangerous a location. So the mother, who was an Aid for Dependent Children (AFDC) recipient, found another apartment, borrowed $300 for the security deposit, and borrowed additional money to move her belongings and her other two children. But before she signed the lease, she had the home health care agency come out to see the neighborhood and to agree to provide care at this location.

She moved to the new location, her child's return home was scheduled, but the home health care agency refused to provide care there, despite a previous commitment to do so. The nurse at the pediatric nursing home called our project to see if there was something we could do about this situation. Happily, there was something we could do, and as a result, the child is home today. But the bad news is, that the pediatric nurse later told us that the HMO went back to that pediatric nursing home and indicated that they may not be willing to place new patients there as long as that nurse remains employed at the facility. The only reason we were able to help that family was because of that nurse advocate, and that nurse advocate may be fired because she advocated on behalf of her patient.

Increasingly, patients are losing their health care providers as advocates. I have never understood why, as an attorney, it is a conflict of interest if I have any financial dealings that may in any way be a conflict of interest with my client, but, it is absolutely all right for a doctor to have a financial conflict of interest with a patient. Many HMO contracts intentionally create a financial incentive for the doctor to deny patients' medically necessary care, which results in some doctors denying, delaying, or avoiding those who most need the care—the most costly patients. Why is it grounds for disbarment in my profession, but perfectly acceptable in the health care profession?

Thus the increased vulnerability of patients. First, their health care is governed by a contract to which they were not a party and which they may not legally be permitted to enforce. Second, they've lost their physicians and other health care providers as their advocates. They are often left alone to fight these billion-dollar managed care corporations.

The first time that many of them come into contact with the HMO is at time of enrollment. Under the proposals before Congress many Medicare and Medicaid beneficiaries are going to be able to be exposed to individual marketing by HMO sales representatives. Often those sales representatives have performance requirements and are on commission. We have handled a number of cases of Medicare recipients who had no idea they were enrolling in an HMO and that their health care costs would not be covered if they went to their usual physicians. Thereafter they went to their usual physician, and received care for such expensive care as cataract operations, hospitalization for strokes, and so on, and then came to us when they were about to lose their homes because the HMO wouldn't pay for the care because they didn't go through their gatekeeper: the primary care physician.

Medicare and Medicaid recipients are going to be particularly vulnerable under managed care. They often have chronic health care problems. HMOs will make money by reducing the care they received under fee for service. Denials of care may be made because the procedure is deemed experimental or not medically necessary. Often patients won't know that they are being denied care because their doctors won't tell them about it.

Too often a patient needs a lawyer and an independent medical expert to obtain health care through the HMO grievance process. Most patients cannot afford to pay an attorney and medical expert to prove medical necessity issues at an HMO grievance proceeding. Who's out there protecting the consumer? Who's out there protecting the patient?

The state is required to monitor HMO operations. However, the state offices charged with this responsibility are terribly understaffed. Staffing has not kept pace with the growth in the industry, and state oversight can be subject to political pressures.

What can be done? In my opinion, the HMO industry needs to be regulated to protect the consumer. HMO marketing and enrollment activities need to be regulated. The inappropriate financial incentives between HMOs and health care providers can't be hidden in contracts where none of us can see them. They must be publicly disclosed, publicly debated, and if they're inappropriate, they've got to be prohibited.

The reviews that are done by independent outside entities need to be made public. Patients have a need to know how their health care plan failed in those reviews. In Pennsylvania, this information is denied to the public because it may contain "trade secrets."

The state needs to require some minimum medical service ratios. There needs to be some limit put on HMO profit, especially if funded by public monies under Medicaid and Medicare. Without these requirements we cannot be sure that enough resources actually go into care and we will continue to hear the patient horror stories that are described in this book. The state needs to fund independent consumer resources, including ombudspersons, consumer advocates, and independently produced consumer report cards. Without these protections, the consumer doesn't stand a chance against the HMOs.

And finally, we need to have health care providers be the patients' advocates for care.

I urge all readers to speak out and to fight practices and policies that keep you from being patient advocates or which would place you in a conflict of interest with your patient.

CHAPTER 11

The Political Aftermath of Health Care Reform

Sidney Blumenthal

The debate about health care going on in Washington, which is at the center of the impasse over the budget, flows from the very debate that took place from 1993 through 1994 and led to the election of this Congress. We are not operating in a vacuum, or with a spontaneous generation of issues. Politics very much will be a determining factor, not only in the outcome of this debate, but will also be a determining factor, over the years, in the very shape of the health care system itself.

We are not dealing with a static system. It is a system that is going to change dramatically in response to politics, not simply markets. And, in that debate, the means of communication are very important, as they have been in the previous debate that took place over the Clinton health care plan. In this chapter, I will briefly discuss what happened to that plan in terms of communications, what is going on now, and what the future might look like.

The Clinton plan was a moderate centrist plan. It was not a lurch to the left. It was not a dramatic proposal of a national health care system,

81

as was proposed in Britain at the end of World War II. It reflected the political realities of the situation, where it was impossible politically to propose other than the system that he proposed, which also made it ideally vulnerable to attack.

Its virtue, the very way it was constructed, was also its flaw. So what the Clintons faced was something they didn't expect, and that is, a massive concerted conservative assault. This debate didn't take place much out in the country. It took place to a great degree in political society centered in Washington. It is a Washington game. And in that game, the conservatives have built up, over the last few decades, tremendous resources that are not matched on the other side.

Though the conservatives whine about the overwhelming liberal eastern establishment media, the fact is that they have constructed a communications machine themselves. This machine involves talk radio and magazines, such as the "American Spectator" and now the Rupert Murdoch-financed "Weekly Standard." It involves newspapers, such as the Moonie-subsidized *Washington Times*, which is the bulletin board for the right wing in Washington and plays a very important role in injecting stories, often not factually based, into the bloodstream of politics. Then, of course, there is *The Wall Street Journal* editorial page, which plays the role of the thunderer on the right. And all of this has had a tremendous effect on the sitting press corps in Washington, which has been borne along in this conservative drift.

This press corps is quite different from the one that is described in Ben Bradlee's joyous memoir. Those days are long gone—the heroic days of "All the President's Men." Instead, we have in Washington today a kind of squalid big casino left over from the 1980s.

You can see the outward flickering manifestations of it on the Friday night, Saturday night, and Sunday morning talk shows; and if you can get on the talk shows, then you can get the lecture fees. There is a kind of Social Darwinism that goes on in the press corps to try and get a piece of this action. This grasping constructs a very different kind of status system and distribution of rewards in Washington.

The conservatives attacked the Clinton plan for being big government, for being nothing but a bureaucracy, for taking away choice, benefits, options, for being a big-spending plan—although, in fact, it would reduce costs greatly. And the attack also took on a personal character. It was called Rodhamism. There was a clearly misogynist element in this attack in which the First Lady was held up to derision. And all of the vulnerabilities of a woman in public life were very carefully exploited by the right in their attack on health care.

At the same time, there was an attack on the character of the President. This took place on a broad front, and no one should doubt that one of the objects of this attack was health care. This attack ginned up precisely after the President made his speech before the joint session of Congress proposing his health care plan. That is when the Whitewater business got inflated, ballooned.

I happen to believe that Whitewater is a nonscandal and is, in fact, a dirty trick. If you look at it from that point of view, you might actually get a story and find something; but since most of the press is not looking at it from that point of view—they have sought to look at it as a scandal—they have not found anything.

All of that combined to create turbulence and negativity around a plan that in the beginning was widely but shallowly approved; to a plan that was, in the end, not even voted upon by the Congress, never brought to the floor. Now, there were a lot of other reasons and factors, but many of them had to do with this communications disequilibrium, this imbalance. The Clintons had on their side consultants; they had slogans. But this was hardly balanced.

The Clintons also had something working against them, which was simply the press of unexpected events entering into the situation, always changing the story line: NAFTA has to be debated and discussed. In October of 1993, Somalia and Haiti happened, and so on, all through the year. That's what always happens to a President. I know that someone from a previous White House had warned the Clintons that about 80 percent of their time would be taken up in firefighting on events that they never would expect, and that's what happens when you're in the White House.

The great consequence of this was that the press fell into an antipolitical mode. It began a denigration of politics. It lacked a historical perspective. Its objectivity, in my view, was debased so that ideological claims of the right were accepted as fact, so that all the charges assessed against the Clinton plan were accepted simply as the considered views of one side that had merit and must be reported as though they were fact. It's a big government plan, for example. It's a big spending plan. He's a tax-and-spender, so on and so forth. These are all facts, aren't they?

But it's a false objectivity, I think we can see. What happened then was that the antipolitical tenor of the press, eager to show the corruption of politics itself, fed into the game plan of Newt Gingrich, seeking to overthrow the long Democratic hold over the Congress. It was Gingrich who understood, quite explicitly, the use of antipolitics in his scheme. While the press did not understand, it certainly acted indirectly as an agent for these forces coming to power in November 1994.

Now we face a very interesting Congress. This is a Congress that harkens back, as was pointed out, to the nineteenth century, and it does so every day in very specific ways. We can look at the story that has been exposed recently involving—and the story is still unfolding—3,400 pages, I'm told, of documents now gotten by the Federal Election Commission showing Newt Gingrich's use of GOPAC (Republican Party Political Action Committee). They show how he used the money not only personally, for his own political gain, but for making deals with very specific interests. That is what is going on in committee after committee in this Congress, and I say this without any hyperbole, but in a very empirical way. That is simply how business is being done. It was not done in this kind of coarse way before.

In the Republicans' health plan, the question of what is in it is determined by which interest prevails and who makes the best deal with the leadership, just as on every other issue. This is not exactly a free market, but it might be something like fee for service.

The innovative role is played by Gingrich's pollster, a young man named Frank Luntz, who was Ross Perot's pollster and, before that, Pat Buchanan's pollster. He's a person of eclectic tastes. Luntz is the one who devised the idea of exploiting the scare over Medicare. As we all may know, there have been nine audits of the Medicare system since it's been founded, which showed that its solvency always needs to be restored, meaning that you need simply to deal with the finances. This is not a crisis. But seizing on the Trustees' report, the Republicans trumpeted a new crisis that required solvency to be restored or else senior citizens would be deprived of their Medicare and, therefore, it must be cut greatly in order to have our version of a balanced budget.

And so the entire Republican plan flows from the defeat of health care. The very existence of the 104th Congress is a consequence of that defeat, and now their budget plan rests on this Medicare presumption of a routine projection of distant insolvency as crisis and the attack, as was pointed out, on Medicaid. Nothing in the Republican numbers work unless they can make those numbers work.

Now, the press has played an odd role in this debate. There have been continuing attacks on the Clintons for this, blaming them for their political errors in not succeeding in passing health care. There has been acceptance of the conservative assumptions, unquestioningly, that there is a crisis of insolvency, even though the Trustees, who are cabinet members, such as the Secretary of the Treasury, Robert Rubin; Secretary of Labor, Robert Reich; Secretary of Health and Human Services, Donna Shalala, have held a press conference and issued a statement saying that this has been vastly distorted and used for political purposes. And elements of the press then have assumed the pose of objectivity to show that both sides are seeking to scare senior citizens, and what this shows above all is the superior objective position of the press.

Now, what's going to happen? I can't tell you what will happen in this particular debate, but what I can say is that there will be consistently new rounds of convulsive political conflicts over the issue of health care. It has been at the center of our politics throughout the 1990s, and it will not fade. It will not be resolved. This conflict will continue to build.

If the Republicans hold the Congress in the next election, there will be assaults on the health care system the likes of which we have not imagined. If they are held off in this current round, it is possible that the President will propose new, although smaller, reforms, even in 1996. I would not be shocked if he tried to do this again and to keep this battle going. But one thing I think is quite clear, and that is that these battles are going to be convulsive and unsettled for a long time to come. And they involve more, I believe, than the abandonment of the patient, because the patient is in a larger sense the citizen. So this is a challenge not simply about the care of the patient, but the notion of citizenship as it has developed over more than the past 50 years.

It was pointed out that there's an attack on the entitlement to health care. That is an attack on a settled right for senior citizens and for the less fortunate. That is considered now, and built into our social structure as a right; and we are at the point now where we are battling over, not simply the abandonment of rights, but the taking of rights.

I also think that there is one other factor, which I'll mention briefly, which is about to come into play in our politics for the long term and has just begun to be visible, and that is quite relevant, I believe, above all, to people in a profession like nursing.

People talk about the gender gap. Well, I believe we're just beginning to see the gender gap, and that has to do with a biological phenomenon, which is that women of my age are, in a very short time, about to turn 50. Baby Boom women are about to turn 50. Just the beginning edge of that Baby Boom is going to start passing that age. And they are the most educated generation of women ever. They're quite capable, as we've all seen, and they're also about to be free of their children and have a little more time. Many of them have disposable incomes. They are the most progressive element in the electorate. And they are about to discover that health care is the issue that concerns them most of all, passing the age of 50.

So we are about to enter into a very different kind of politics at the same time that health care has entered the center of convulsive politics in the 1990s.

CHAPTER 12

Do Ethics and Money Mix? The Moral Implications of the Corporatization of Health Care

Arthur Caplan

ecently, I consulted on a situation at the Children's Hospital of Philadelphia that involved abandonment of the patient, not by people at Children's, but by other people in the system. It was a very interesting and sad case, which I will describe, along with other aspects related to abandoning the American patient. At the same time, I will include some thoughts about both what structural features exist that lead to abandonment and some things that we may need to do to resolve and respond to these problems.

We must begin by analyzing what the symptoms or signs are that a patient in the American health care system is in trouble. The case I mentioned above involved a young boy who has cystic fibrosis. He was at Children's Hospital for a workup to be considered a candidate for a new form of treatment—gene therapy for cystic fibrosis. But, that isn't the cause of his abandonment. Nine months ago, his mother died of breast cancer. She had had the diagnosis for about a year before her death, so she knew she was dying and she had received treatment. In the months before her death, the family had received, in the home, which is up in Montgomery County just north of Philadelphia, home health care. A home care nurse had come to the home, given her medicines, and done other functions to support the mother as she died. The day after she died, the home care nurse was pulled from the house.

There are three children in the family. One is a young boy of ten, who has attention deficit disorder and other severe behavioral troubles. He takes certain drugs to control this. The other boy has cystic fibrosis, and he needs a variety of medications and treatments. When the mom died, the dad was left with the three kids, two of whom have medical conditions that need either licensed nurses or doctors to give them their medicines. When the family called the managed care company, which was the third-party payer, that organization said that since the person had been there to treat the mom and the mom was dead, there was no reason for them to be in the house.

This left the father faced with the prospect of quitting his job or getting fired, going onto Medicaid and having the state pay for an aide, if that provider could be covered under Medicaid, which is a whole other song and dance about how long that might take. Basically, this father, in the middle of his problems and grief over his dead wife, is trying to make funeral arrangements while also trying to figure out what to do with these two kids with health problems.

It seems as if that problem might just be laid at the foot of the current fiscal and management strategies that we have. But I don't think so. I don't think it was actually any better 10 or 20 years ago. The system hasn't ever been especially kind with respect to chronic and long-term problems and home health care needs, and it is not now. But that doesn't mean that it is any less important to do something about it now. The issues of what to do about follow-up, long-term care, and family support remain.

If we are going to shift how we pay and finance health care and how we deliver it, then those questions now belong appropriately on the plate of the new providers and payers. They can't escape them just because it wasn't done right before.

Whenever I meander toward the Wharton School, I fall under the radiant splendor of exposition by economists. Economists are fine people. One of the things many of them believe in very strongly is that there is no better way than the market to resolve problems of cost, allocation, and distribution. It is clear that this country currently has decided to turn to market mechanisms with a vengeance to solve its main problem of health care, which is not the abandonment of the patient. The number one problem is, simply, to contain cost. Period. End of discussion. That's it. That is what the policy objective is, and that is all anybody wants to talk about.

The difficulty with using the market to do that is well exemplified by the plight of the City of Cleveland. The City of Cleveland doesn't, or soon won't, have a football team. The people of the City of Cleveland are very angry about this and, indeed, much to my absolute incredulity, the City sent its two Senators, one of whom is a pretty conservative Republican, to submit legislation to forbid NFL teams from being able to move where the money is. This would allow NFL teams an exemption from antitrust legislation of the sort that baseball has. And, what does this have to do with health care? It has everything to do with health care.

Why are people in Baltimore and Houston and Cleveland and, for a while, Oakland and now Los Angeles, upset about football? What's going on is a very simple demonstration of market failure. The market is basically saying, if you have a team and we have the money, we'll move your team. There is no such thing as loyalty, as fidelity, as a sense of community, as a sense of trust. Those four features are what might be called virtues, a kind of funny old term that we don't talk about much in public anymore, unless we're going to some kind of religious meeting. But the fact is that virtues and values are not always something that you can achieve by means of market mechanism distribution.

The clearest example is professional sports in America. People are angry at the idea that the players aren't loyal to the town; that there's no continuity in the membership of the teams; that the teams can pick up and leave them holding the bag at a moment's notice. But it is a well-run market. What's wrong? There are resources, people with money; they compete and it's distributed, but it doesn't give us what we want, or at least what many people want. Well, if it doesn't work in sports team distribution, then why have we committed ourselves to it being the only mechanism of distribution for health care?

The NFL exemption from antitrust is something the Senate would never consider passing for health care. How can that be? Is health care something that doesn't require more virtue than the Houston Oilers? Is that possible? I doubt it. But it's a good example of the market driving thing—causing distributions and, possibly, directing the delivery of care in ways that we don't like, with people who lack the virtues of loyalty, advocacy, fidelity, and community. That, I think, is why people feel that the patient is being abandoned.

Some of the things we've come to expect from nurses, doctors, administrators, and hospitals aren't there anymore, because they're up for grabs. Maybe the big outsider can come in and buy the system. Maybe there's no sense of community in the institution anymore. Maybe the physicians will be moved around to the highest-priced bidder, or maybe the administrators will move the nurses or fire them, depending upon how they want to cut cost at any given time. It is a pretty grim picture if it is really nothing more than an unregulated market.

In the meantime, what are we doing about home care, long-term care, and those problems? In my opinion, while people feel unhappy about their acute care setting, where they are abandoned most is at home. They're not worried so much about being abandoned in the emergency room, but they are worried about being left with two children who have health problems in their house, with a recently deceased spouse. That's a problem.

A second worry is being abandoned—just like they worry about their football team picking up and leaving them. They worry that the big, nasty health care conglomerate will buy their hospital and shut it. And that would be to abandon them.

A third way in which they're worried is about the closure of systems. I experienced this in Minnesota before I came to Philadelphia. I had the opportunity to watch managed care come to a state and end up controlling a huge percentage of all patient care. Now, there is nothing but managed care in Minnesota. When I first was in the state in 1987, there were twelve HMOs. There are now four. There will soon be three, and I wouldn't be surprised if soon after that there are two.

In fact, those of you who favor national health care need only wait for a while. There will probably be one big HMO after a time, and then you can seize it and do what was proposed by Beven to create the British

National Health Service, just socialize the one remaining thing left standing.

I do believe that if you don't regulate this market, the result is oligopoly. It is not to make sure that pure competition will endure. It won't. I've seen it collapse. I have seen HMOs belly-up because they were undercapitalized and leave entire counties with no provider because there was no minimal restriction on who was there and what they were doing. As a result, there was no one delivering care for a whole year across a set of counties in Northern Minnesota, because there wasn't much regulation, control, and oversight of what was going on.

Another problem is exemplified by one case that involved an experimental procedure that someone needed. At this large conglomerate HMO, where I sat in at the board meeting, the procedure came up and the manager said, "Well, Mr. Smith needs a, you know, jujajectomy-waffleotomy-something and it's experimental and there's only been three done in the world and, gosh, we don't have to pay for that. We don't even know if it's going to work and it's terrible." The first question was, "Does Mr. Smith have a lawyer?" The second question was, "Is Mr. Smith articulate?" And the third question was, "Is Mr. Smith likely to cause a problem if we turn him down?" The answers were all "yes" and Mr. Smith got his coverage. Although that is not a very good way to make coverage decisions, that is the way that a lot of them get made.

I write a newspaper column (Caplan, 1995b). Through writing this column, I have bullied a couple of HMOs into providing coverage for people. But is that a fair way to get coverage? If somebody writes a column about them or some TV station chases them down the street and forces, through publicity or the threat of bad publicity, U.S. Healthcare, or Blue Cross, or whoever it is, to provide coverage, that's not fair to the people who don't want to go public or don't have access to those outlets and, it isn't going to work in the long run because after a time, the media get tired of running stories about patients who can't get coverage. So that is not a good system for determining what ought to be covered. It is a major source of people feeling abandoned because they don't know what their coverage will be.

Patients are abandoned at home, abandoned in the sense of losing their providers or losing what made their providers attractive to them in terms of their virtues, and abandoned in terms of coverage uncertainty. Those are all problems of patient abandonment in the current system. And the last area of abandonment is abandonment when they die.

There have been about four papers that have come out recently which are staggering and startling in their implications for why people feel abandoned when they die. The major story is a large, multimillion-dollar study, funded by a consortium of foundations (Support, *JAMA* 1995). Called "The Support Study," it looked at five acute care hospitals, affiliated with teaching institutions around the country. The investigators studied what happened as people die. They were interested in finding out if people had living wills or advanced directives; did they, in fact, get do-not-resuscitate (DNR) orders, or no-CPR orders when they wanted them; did they spend time comatose in the ICU before they died, if so, how long, and is that something they wanted; and, did they feel they had good communication with their health care providers during the entire process?

The empirical part of the study occurred in the identified intensive care unit settings and, indeed, people (or their survivors) reported that they did not get anything they wanted, and that they experienced a lot of discontent. These findings led to the second phase of the study. In this phase, the investigators retained a nurse to have discussions with the doctors, the patients and their families about advanced directives, about CPR, about DNR, about what an intensive care unit is like, about what it is like to try and make your wishes known with respect to aggressive care. All the patients in the study were diagnosed with very serious illnesses, and believed to have six months or less to live.

The study found that the nurses' discussion and teaching about all the options made no difference. The same problems occurred with or without the educational program presented by the nurse: People don't have living wills. They're still getting resuscitated when they don't want to be. They've spent exactly the same amount of time comatose, 7, 8 days, before they died in the ICU with or without living wills and other advanced directives regarding how they wish to die.

If you ever want to see a case for abandonment, watch people rally to Dr. Kevorkian. He would be attractive to nobody with any rational sense unless there was something worse out there, and there is. The system can't figure out how to turn off the spigot when people are dying. And, the saddest conclusion in these studies is that we should just try harder with living wills and advanced directives.

Now, let me tell you, the chances of the system hiring a nurse to go talk to patients and families as people die, and putting the resources into that, is zero. It is not the direction the system is going in. If a multimillion-dollar level of intervention didn't get people to fill out a living will and get doctors to pay attention to it and get family members to be comfortable with it, the proper conclusion is, forget it. That is not the road to success. This approach will not work, so let's come up with new ideas. Then the question becomes, what else have we got? And that is the last aspect of abandonment that I want to discuss.

Basically, people are fearful about two things: that they will be abandoned to a technology that they don't want or, conversely, that they will be abandoned prematurely by people who wield this technology, who don't see them as worthy of the effort. In the case of the poor and minorities, they fear they will be killed prematurely. Considering the amount of money the system spends on dying people, it is staggering how little is our level of trust about how we die (Caplan, 1994a).

If cost is the problem and we're worried about abandonment in the setting of cost, then the question is, is managed care the answer for us in its present form? This question invites some comment about what some of the problems are when you let the marketplace alone, unregulated, unsupervised, and unaccountable, to run health care. You are going to have full-bore market competition with zero accountability to anybody. There isn't even the equivalent of the Pennsylvania Boxing Commission to supervise Don King; not even the appearance of somebody looking over somebody's shoulder; absolutely nothing in place at the federal level or at the state level.

The problem now in managed care is this: Number one, the abandoned patients in the managed care setting, knowing that cost is driving the system, worry that they're going to lose their choice of doctor; that continuity of care will fall apart; that they will also lose their confidentiality and privacy. They are correct to worry about all these things.

There is a bill in front of Congress now, which is going under the title of the Federal Privacy Protection Statute, but might better be described as the Anybody Who Wants to Can Look at Your Medical Records Statute. This bill will absolutely put the final nail in the coffin of privacy and confidentiality in this system. The patient in the managed care system that has evolved up until this point in time is basically being told, you are going to have to go with the systems that we give you. You are going to have to go with the providers that your employer thinks are worth contracting with; and, in many instances, you will have to live with the doctor that is given to you; and, if that doctor leaves the system, then you'll just have to take the next one. And you are going to have to turn over to us all information about your mental health, sexual history, physical well being, and genetic tests, so we can make sure that your care is worth paying for.

There are some pretty tough privacy laws on the books right now. Yet, the first thing a patient signs upon entering a clinic, hospital, or nursing home is a complete waiver to turn over all information to third-party payors. So privacy is gone, too, which is another source of complete abandonment of patient autonomy under this style of managed care.

The second problem of managed care has to do with provider motivation. Under the old fee for service system, the basic approach was to make a lot of money by doing more things, which had its ethical problems, but at least one thing the patient could believe was that if the clinician was going to make a mistake, they were going to make a mistake in the direction of giving you too much.

Under managed care, the incentives have shifted to worry about under-treatment. It's a problem for patients but it's also a major problem for providers because their notion of fidelity, of trustworthiness is based on the idea that they will be good advocates. If someone is your advocate, then you assume they will do what they can to secure resources for you. If managed care makes the clinician a gatekeeper, as well as the advocate, then the advocacy role collapses. In the final analysis the real problem with managed care is that the cost containment approach, in its present form, means that you can't trust your doctor or nurse anymore. In fact, you do not trust anybody in this system because they are your gatekeepers.

The current arrangement, without something being changed, leads to the collapse of trust between doctor and patient, nurse and patient, health care provider and patient. And those are the two major problems with managed care: loss of choice, loss of control from the patient side; loss of trust, loss of fidelity from the provider side.

What should be done? We do need to do what President Clinton began thinking about in his health care reform effort. There has to be a clear values message that guides health care. If the values message is simply to contain cost, then you really could just cut out programs. But, if you want something more, then you have to articulate a values mission, that is, state what the system should do besides save money. You might say that you want a system that gives people choice or continuity or portability or quality or fair access or a floor of basic coverage that they can feel peace of mind about. Those are, I think, the sales points of health reform and, indeed, the sales points of trying to regulate managed competition. Oddly enough, with all due respect to my friends in the world of economics, the only way to regulate this market is to stand ethical values up against it—not to let the market run unbridled and impress people with the latest cost curve projection. Individuals involved will have to stand up and say, what should this health care system do? What values do we want it to serve? And then try and sell this to people. The restrictions, buffers, oversighting, and accountability that must be put on the market system to make sure that it meets those other goals aside from saving money must be examined. If you just tell the market to save money, which is the message that has been sent so far, then you are going to get the kind of slashing and hacking of programs on the federal side, and the unbridled competition on the private sector side, that we have got right now.

The benefits coverage decision-making process that I described earlier must be replaced by community-involved boards and panels that will make coverage decisions about what plans should do. There are plans that do this. Consumers sit with the medical director, and somebody from the administration, and they actually say, this year, we are going to pay for that or we're not going to pay for this and here's why. And, if you disagree with this, here's what it would cost in terms of premiums and you can throw us all off the board if you don't like it.

Further, there should be a political mechanism put in place to make sure that every coverage decision is accountable by a plan. Related to that, we should not have any less oversight for the health care industry than we have got for communications, power, electricity, or water.

There is nothing intrinsically wrong with trying to make money from health care, but it has to honor the idea that, just as everybody is supposed to get some water, and everybody's supposed to be able to get a telephone, everybody ought to be able to get some health care. It is a public utility approach to health care (Caplan, 1992).

In addition, there ought to be some minimal financial standards: How much money should these plans have to have in the bank? How much money can they build up before they have to spend some? (This has been a problem in some parts of the country.) Are there reserves beyond which the plan must cycle monies back into the system to allow more coverage, or can they just save the money forever? (Some plans are getting perilously close to doing this right now.) What can you do to prevent the small plan from being pushed out of the marketplace completely? The nation has worried about the plight of small companies in the airline industry, trying to make niches for small competitors to come in, and we can worry about it in the same way here.

In other words, it seems that thinking about how we handle utilities such as oil, telephone, gas, and even, to some extent, the supply of food and education, with its community boards and its school boards, will tell us something about what can be done with a crucial resource like health care. What people believe, and what Americans will buy about health care is that there ought to be a decent minimum available to all. There should be a floor. The ceiling can be as high as anybody wishes to make it.

We don't have to get into a discussion about what we allow people to do with their disposable income in regard to health care any more than we do with their vacation homes or how many trips they want to take or where they live. But we do have to get into a discussion of what is the decent minimum. Decent minimum is the proper way to talk and it relates to the other reason that health care is important.

Health care is important because, at this point in time, it is a basic opportunity enhancer. People can't compete in the marketplace unless—and this is particularly true for children and young people—you have access to health care to give you opportunity. If you are disabled, if you are impaired, if you are sick, if you wind up less able to speak, hear, ambulate, and so forth, then you are put at a disadvantage. You do not have equal opportunity. Americans don't care for pure egalitarianism, but they are interested in equal opportunity, where everybody should get their shot. And whatever political persuasion you hold, both Democrat and Republican or Socialist or Libertarian, the opportunity option is the correct value to argue for the decent minimum. It is the value that should be buffering the marketplace approach to health care. It is the thing we want the health care system to do. We want effective care to go to people who, whether they can pay for it or not, will benefit from it because it enhances their life opportunities (Caplan, 1992).

The last areas I will discuss are about dying. The big expenditure of money at the time of death, and the true meanings people attach to dying that have nothing to do with how we manage it. Dying has nothing to do with lawyers. It probably has nothing to do with doctors. It has a lot to do with the things on that list of funny little virtues discussed earlier in this chapter, things like faithfulness, and trust, and loyalty (Caplan, 1994b).

If you go to the ICU and watch people die, what you will notice is that it is a time when families try to reconcile. It is a time when people build their self-image about whether they are fighters or tough. It is a time when people begin to think about whether they are going to linger on because they want to redeem their lives or because they feel that they ought to suffer for their sins. They want to do things like expiate their existence on this Earth. And, there are plenty of clinicians who are pretty handy with a nasogastric tube in the ICU, but there is nobody who is very handy with any of the concepts listed above.

We have giant temples of high towers, surrounded by our favorite technologies which we say we hate, but we clearly do not, by people who are afraid to shut them off because they're not sure, symbolically, what that means. And what it means, literally, is abandonment. Abandonment by whom? By the family of the loved one.

If a clinician approaches a family and tells them, ''There's a living will here and I need your permission before I can shut off the ventilator on Mr. X,'' it's a pretty crusty person who can say, ''Okay, I'll kill Pop. Shut it off.'' I've never seen a parent do it with a child. If you go to parents and say, ''Look, Johnny's sick and there's a one-in-a-million chance that anything can happen beneficial to Johnny''—the Lakeberg twins are a recent example. There's a one-in-a-million chance we could do anything to separate these twins and save them, one in a million. Well, in decision theory, no one's going to take that. But mothers do. What mother isn't going to take a one-in-a-million chance to save her child? But that's the system we've got in place. It basically says who you are. How you die, how you define your guilt, your responsibility, your ability to redeem yourself is being played out in a very expensive place with concepts in play that almost nobody is willing to talk about or discuss.

Recommendations to redirect the system might include giving incentives for dying people to go someplace else, more hospice, more home care, better nursing homes, to move the dying person away from the technological solutions that don't meet their needs as they die. You don't have to go to an ICU to prove to us that you are tough or a fighter or a real person or virtuous. You can go to the hospice and we will be just as proud of you and you will be as proud of yourself. We will talk to you about what it means to feel bad or guilty that you haven't seen dad for ten years. But coming here, making him live another month, vomiting and attached to a machine, is not necessarily a sign of affection. We could set the system up differently, and better, if we would admit that dying has to do with symbolism, spirituality, and religion.

We might even do a better job if we could actually get our religious organizations and groups to feel more comfortable about dying. One of the odd things about America is, it seems consumed with religious discussion these days, except in one place, where people die. There, there's almost nobody with religious training, background, ever around. In the seminary and the other religious organizations, we are not training our rabbis and priests and ministers and mullahs to deal well with counseling and bereavement and pastoral care. But they are the places to which we should be turning, not to lawyers.

Having a lawyer-doctor mix, by the way, as part of the last act of your dying, is true American optimism that flabbergasts me. Somebody once said to me, ''Well, I made out a living will and I left it with my lawyer, so I know that it's in good shape.'' I just say ''Well, okay. So you're dying and who is the last person your doctor's going to call?'' It's just not the way to go.

But dying and death are very symbolic. They are very spiritual. They are very religious. They are psychological. They're emotional. They're all the things that the health care system isn't too good at. That's why people feel abandoned as they die. It makes them feel so abandoned that what they're trying to do is get the right to be killed before they have to go to an ICU, which has to be one of the strangest occurrences in the history of modern America. On the one hand, we state that there must be something better than the way we die now and, on the other hand, we come to the recognition that the only solution we can get to before we create a right to health care is a right to euthanasia. However, we are very close to having that. One state, Oregon, has passed a right to euthanasia that doesn't have a right to health care.

Our health care system is fraught with problems, from its lack of continuity of care, to its inability to move outside its hospital setting, to its inability to come up with a better way to push for cost containment, all the way through to its inability to approach how we die (Caplan, 1995a). I've offered some suggestions about ways in which public and community involvement, locally, in the form of utility regulation and, to some extent, through civic and church organizations and their training, might help us get at this problem of abandonment.

Despite my somewhat cynical tone, I actually think things can be done. Abandonment is the worst moral sin that people can accuse a medical professional of committing. There is nothing worse. You are never supposed to abandon your patient. Once you have them, you stay with them. But if our structural, economic, cultural, and spiritual context creates the feeling of abandonment, then we are committing a grave sin that should be rectified through the implementation of some of these proposed solutions.

CHAPTER 13

Conclusion: What Can We Do to Protect Quality Care?

—— Claire M. Fagin and Suzanne Gordon ——

The preceding chapters make it clear that the patients and families who rely on the health care system, and those of us who have devoted our lives to ensuring quality care to patients and families, face momentous issues. The pendulum has swung from the "never mind the cost" philosophy of two decades ago to the bottom-line philosophy of today. Health care providers, long sheltered by third-party cost reimbursement policies, are now facing the specter of cost competition. The anticipated congressional cap on Medicare and Medicaid will exacerbate the scramble to devise strategies to compete. We are already seeing the influence of for-profit managed care and home health care companies driving the not-for-profits out of the market, or causing them to bring down costs in order to stay in business.

Many of the preceding chapters link the abandonment of the patient to the corporatization of health care. The original concept of managed care aimed to help the patient negotiate the increasingly complex world of health care and change the focus of care to prevention, coordination of services, and the like. Managed care is now more and more likely to mean cost control and cost reduction. The fallout includes overloaded and undertrained care givers, patients' early discharge from hospitals to inadequate home care, and less choice, more out of pocket cost, and reduced access to health care for all people. And, the direct effect of a cap on Medicare and Medicaid is yet to be felt.

Every health care system must manage care, indeed, must ration care. But the operative word, principle, and philosophy must be *care*, not *profit*. For this reason, we challenge those who are in the business of managing cost to focus on the stories presented in these chapters. They are disturbing and must not be ignored.

We believe, with many others, that managed care organizations can ultimately offer the most promising solution to the nation's health care problems. Coordination of care has always been a problem in traditional, acute-care focused medicine. Too much care—that is, unnecessary or inappropriate care—not only has cost money, but has made patients vulnerable to harmful side effects. As the population ages, the needs of patients coupled with accelerating health costs necessitate a system of care that provides better coordination, less fragmentation, awareness of the complete health record, preventive services, and education. While many of us might personally prefer fee-for-service arrangements, which offer us wide choices paid for by generous health benefit plans, there is little evidence that, in the aggregate, these expensive packages of benefits are any more effective at assuring quality than is appropriately managed care.

But there is the rub: what is appropriately managed care? No system changing as fast as health care delivery can be all good, or all safe, or all of even quality. How is the consumer to have any idea of what to look for, or how to evaluate what they are getting, without a regular source of information and support? And, how will people be able to maintain their trust in their health care providers and the institutions that have merited their respect for almost a century?

It is clear that many professionals are skeptical about the marketplace invasion of health care. We are deeply concerned because we do not believe that industrial models of care and treatment should be applied to the sick and vulnerable—or to the healthy who, after all, use the health care system because they fear sickness and vulnerability.

Despite its prevalence, managed care is, in many respects, in its infancy, and we need new research and data to offer pioneering new directions with the potential to shape health care reform. We need our clinical researchers to tell us what evaluations are revealing about the rapid changes of restructuring and shifting of modalities for health care delivery. We need clinical researchers to investigate and uncover best practices. We need to know about the post-hospital experiences of patients who do not have expert care. We need to know the steps managed care organizations are taking to adapt their services to the older or poorer, and often less healthy, populations they are seeking to attract currently.

If the marketplace believes that competition is the solution to the health care crisis of this nation, then it must create a system that competes on quality. But that is not what we have today. If the HMO and insurer's real customer is the employer who purchases health care, not the employee who uses it, then there is no competition in health care. If the users of health care services do not have freedom of choice of provider, hospital, nursing home, subacute facility, or home care agency, then there is no competition in health care. Let's be truthful in our discussion. How can there be competition in health care when the majority of employers who offer health benefits offer no choice of health care plan? How can we claim we are delivering genuine health care in a competitive system when employees who lose faith in an HMO, physician, or hospital are imprisoned in the very institutions they have come to distrust?

Today patient care is being redefined almost entirely in market terms, where cost rather than care has the highest priority. Those governing our health care system advertise quality but, in reality, they profit from the healthy and lose money from caring for the sick.

As we learn in increasingly frequent news reports, the savings corporate managed care is wresting from the health care system are not being redirected toward the long overdue effort to insure the uninsured. Savings are not even being directed to enhancing the delivery of care to those with health insurance. Nor are savings being directed to education and research.

One HMO executive recently expressed his delight to see that the industrial revolution had finally penetrated the health care delivery system. Under HMO direction, he said, physicians would be turned into sophisticated machine tools programmed to deliver the care that his and other managed care companies deem appropriate. Do we really want our health care system to turn patients into predictable units of production and transform nurses and physicians into assembly-line workers or supervisors? Or, do we want a health care system that recognizes illness as the ultimate unpredictable human event and that responds to that need with flexible, individualized models of care delivery?

Today, HMOs, insurers, and hospitals are developing standards of care, algorithms, and critical pathways that determine patients' fates, but are shielded from patient or public scrutiny. In their public pronouncements, health plans insist that guidelines or standards of care are applied flexibly and are tailored to each patient's needs. We know, however, that clinicians who deviate from practice rules are penalized and that financial incentives are used to motivate physicians to provide fewer medical services.

In December, the Center for Health Care Rights in Los Angeles released a 250 page study entitled, "Consumer Protection in State HMO Laws. Volume 1: Analysis and Recommendations" (Dallek, 1995). The study highlights serious concerns about marketing, lack of open enrollment, and contract cancellation periods. It expressed concern about grievance procedures, accountability, HMO lock-in provisions, referral and utilization control systems or delays, and restricted access to care. The study's exhaustive review of state statutes reveals that, "Most states do not provide adequate protections for HMO enrollees. In every area of consumer HMO law, but especially in the areas of access, quality of care, grievance procedures, the collection, analysis and release of quality care data, and the provision of HMO information to enrollees and the public, the study found that critical legal and regulatory issues were not addressed."

Recently the National Health Council (1995) issued a publication which lists their recommendations for consumers in examining managed care options, and the Citizen Action and the Consumers Union released "The Managed Care Consumers' Bill of Rights" (Finkelstein, 1995). Their list of ten fundamental rights are: access, choice, comprehensive benefits, affordability, quality, appeals, representation, and enforcement. All of these groups express grave concern, but are part of a growing cohort of consumer advocates whose actions have the potential to help mold the changing scene.

There are certain requirements that need to be considered as we examine managed care and any other care system offered to the public. The factors listed by the National Health Council Report and the Consumers Bill of Rights are a good starting point. In addition, there must be a "safety net" which would impose and fund minimum standards. It is clear that this is not on the horizon at this time. If we are to protect rather than abandon patients, choice, quality, accountability, and public disclosure should be nonnegotiable.

All recent reports agree on the importance of choice. Americans, like Europeans and Canadians, must have some choice of health care provider, hospital, nursing home, or home care agency. Health care choices must, moreover, include preventive and counseling services, alternatives to hospitalization such as home care, birthing centers, hospice services in the home, residential hospices, and in-patient palliative care units.

We must rigorously debunk the ludicrous notion that people who can switch HMOs once a year have choice. If a person joins a health care plan in January, is diagnosed with pancreatic cancer in March, discovers that he does not trust his doctor, hospital, and health care plan, it is hardly of consolation to learn he can switch plans ten months later, after he may have died.

Second is quality. All of us are concerned about the erosion of quality of care. In 1990, the Institute of Medicine defined quality as the degree to which health services for individuals and populations increase the likelihood of desired health outcomes. Quality is composed of various factors. Among them are core benefits offered, the expertise of practitioners, time spent with patients, appropriate care given in the right place, trust, and access to care (IOM, 1990).

Patients have a right to caregivers who have been educated and licensed because they have mastered the art and science of delivering care. Yet today, patients are increasingly denied access to expert caregivers. Recent assessments of the oversupply of physicians and nurses are based on a variety of factors, some predicted for years and others anticipated only because of managed care companies' rearrangement of physician specialists' and nurses' practices. This linkage is unfortunate. In many institutions, there are artificially induced shortages of *nursing* where care resembles the early 1980s when there was a real shortage of *nurses*.

Time is another element that is critical to the delivery of quality health care. Health professionals cannot deliver adequate health care services if they have no time to get to know their patients or deliver those services. In the hospital, office, and home, practitioners and patients are being denied needed time. For example, at Kaiser in Northern California, family practice physicians now carry patient panels of 2,400 to 2,700 patients. That is 500 to 800 more patients than are on the panel of the British GPs, the most harried generalists in the industrialized world. It is estimated that this patient load will allow for about five minutes per patient–doctor encounter.

Quality of care also means appropriate care given in the right place. We need standards for the combination of hospital stay and home care. Today, the United States has the shortest length of hospital stay of any nation in the industrialized world. Genuine health care does not demand endless, unnecessary hospital stays, but it does demand that length of stay be determined by the doctor, nurse, and patient together. What determines length of stay should be the stability of the patient's condition, the safety of the home or community environment, and the quality of caregiving available outside of the hospital.

Studies conducted at the University of Pennsylvania by nursing professor Dorothy Brooten and others have confirmed the kind of excellent outcomes that are achieved when home care is delivered and monitored by advanced practice nurses (1986; 1994). Indeed, clinical expertise is even more critical in the home than in the hospital. In the hospital, novices or inexperienced workers have at least some hope of finding an expert who they can consult to fill in the gaps of their knowledge. In the home, both patient and caregiver are on their own. To have high quality care in the home, expertise is essential.

But today more and more patients are being sent home too quickly. Once at home, care provided is very short term and the caregivers are more and more likely to be untrained workers. These personnel may be asked to give enemas, insulin shots, change sterile dressings, and hook up complicated machines, to name only a few of the so-called tasks they are assigned.

Care is more and more often assigned to inexperienced family members, most of them women. These family members are further compromised by a society that demands that they take time from work, or sacrifice their jobs entirely, to provide the kind of care that used to be provided in the hospital or in nursing homes. Time must be a focus of our attention as we advocate for the patient.

Trust is also a nonnegotiable of quality care. But trust is being undermined by the kind of economic blackmail that threatens professionals who try to protect quality care or journalists whose employers are concerned about losing advertising revenues or the pernicious economic incentives that reward doctors and administrators for denying needed care. As we are learning daily, physician reimbursement is explicitly linked to the denial of tests, procedures, specialist consultations, and hospital days to patients who need them. New Jersey and New York are revamping HMO regulations to uncover these practices. When caregivers are encouraged to view the sick as a burden—as the "medical loss ratio"—then one can only conclude that care is being managed right out of health care.

Quality health care also demands that patients have access to services when they need them. Instead, the frantic effort to contain costs has turned access into an exercise in corporate gamesmanship. Consider the extraordinary phenomenon of the retrospective denial of emergency room services. A patient experiences crushing chest pain. Fearful that he is having a heart attack, he rushes to the ER. He is worked up and it's discovered that he is not having a heart attack, but rather a bad attack of gastritis. That's the good news. The bad news is that his insurance plan refuses to pay for this medical work-up because he did not have a heart attack. One wonders about the fevered imaginations of those who think up such parameters, but we must be mindful of their result. Patients will fear making a visit to the emergency room because they cannot predict the financial result. Therefore, in essence, the system is requiring of patients the impossible and the unacceptable, that they diagnose their own complex medical conditions.

Third on our list of nonnegotiables is accountability. Today, more and more HMOs are requiring patients to sign away their rights to sue an HMO for malpractice and doctors to sign away their right to hold the HMO accountable for the results of their policies that doctors are asked to enforce. Where is the accountability in such a system? As the new health care system zooms to incorporate itself and all of us, it is crucial that we know about the Review and Regulatory Mechanisms governing it. What are they? Who creates them? Are clinicians and patients part of the process?

The fourth nonnegotiable in the evolving system must be public disclosure, which includes free access to information for patients and providers. Patients and families must have access to information that will allow them to make informed choices. We must pressure for federal, state and local requirements for public accounting. Granted, this is a complex process, but crucial if choice is to have any meaning. Such accounting should include information of the clinical guidelines that are used, and the professional oversight of these guidelines. We ought to know how much of every dollar is spent on clinical personnel, administrative personnel, research, education, indigent care, and overhead. Further, we need information about appeals processes, grievances filed, and results.

At this time most managed care arrangements monitor care, but only some disclose data on quality and cost effectiveness of providers and services. We do know something about overhead though. According to Burner and Waldo (1995), the very successful managed care companies report an overhead of close to 30 percent, as compared with Medicare, which spent 1.74 percent in 1995, and Medicaid, which spent 4.41 percent.

Finally, we cannot think of quality of care while allowing the number of uninsured and underinsured Americans to rise. We must extend coverage to all. The fact that the United States spends more than a trillion dollars on health care per year, more than any other nation in the world, yet has rationed 41 million people right out of the health care system is totally unacceptable. To talk about universal coverage at this time sounds like pie in the sky. Oddly, we believe that in the next five to seven years it will be seen as a necessity, rather than an aspect of altruism. There will be no way for hospitals to manage to care for the indigent, for the uninsured middle class, to educate physicians, or to participate in education of all health care providers, without a concept of universality in health care coverage. Cost shifting is at least moribund, if not dead.

Many strategies for addressing the health care crisis have been addressed in the preceding chapters. The three main thrusts of these strategies are: Publicity, Political Action, and Coalition Building.

Publicity. We must publicize the abandonment of the patient in America. Many of you reading these chapters are already working to protect patients. We hope that those of you whose concern has not yet led to such action will begin to discuss these chapters with associates, friends, and relatives. Add your voices, your stories, your phone calls, and your letters to the media. We need these stories to get a public airing. Journalists are available to report these stories and those of us working with patients need to share our stories with them. Reporters must penetrate the walls of denial and economic blackmail that conceal the facts of what is happening in health and illness care today. The sooner we all act on behalf of patients, the fewer horror stories there will be. We don't want to duplicate the nursing home scandals to get positive results.

Political Action. Every interested person must contact their political representatives about cuts in Medicare and Medicaid. These calls and letters must not be just from health professionals. They must be from the public at large. Health professionals must start educating their friends, families, and colleagues about what is happening in health care. We must get our professional and consumer organizations to besiege our legislative representatives. Members of medical, nursing, social work, and other professional organizations should seek an accounting of what political action those organizations are doing and who they are seeing. Legislators need to know that cost reductions being implemented are being gained at the expense of the patient. Their plans on Medicare and Medicaid will intensify the problem and pierce whatever safety net currently exists. Legislators and regulators will respond to public concern and activism. In Maryland, New Jersey, and Massachusetts, legislators have passed bills to stop what is known as the OB express, and to allow mothers and newborns to stay in the hospital for 48 hours after a normal labor and delivery, if necessary. Similar legislation is being proposed in California, Maine, and other states as well as in Congress. Legislation or regulation is also proposed to curtail the retrospective denial of emergency room services, to publicly expose the practice of giving physicians bonuses for denying needed care, and in many other areas. Clearly, part of any legislative agenda for change must include whistle-blower protection for those employees who speak out to protect the patient. It must also ban the kinds of perverse gag orders and financial incentives that explicitly pit physicians against their patients.

Coalition Building. We need coalitions of health professionals, hospitals, and consumer groups to lobby at every governmental level and to work together to publicize the problems they see. Surely these groups can find common ground among these concerns. Certainly no health professional motivated by altruism and trained to accountability wants to be forced to compete by reducing the quality of health care.

One kind of coalition could be local "watchdog" groups, which would be available to answer questions, monitor care, promote discussion, and debate. At the University of Pennsylvania, colleagues like Anne Torregrossa are developing such a group and involving students in law, medicine, social work, and nursing.

Publicity, political action, and coalition building can become part and parcel of our direct patient care roles as we help our patients advocate for themselves with their own doctors, hospitals, and HMOs, and in the political arena. When we hear patients, friends, family members, and neighbors complain of eroding quality care, we must urge them to call their political representatives, write and complain to state boards of health and insurance, and the chairpeople of their state legislature's health committee, and the media. Those of us who are patients, or represent groups of patients, must work to educate the public and one another about our options, and the remedies available.

In our country, we have great faith in the ability of the marketplace and of competition to serve us and our loved ones. We believe, in spite of evidence to the contrary, that the private sector is more efficient in delivering its products. Perhaps health care is the ultimate testing ground of this mythical faith in the market.

Which is why, in closing, we ask all of us to consider the ultimate issue. When Adam Smith and those who initially developed the ideals of the marketplace and replaced the concept of divine providence with the idea of invisible hand, even they cautioned that the marketplace should be kept in its place and should not invade what they called civil society. Today, those warnings have not been heeded and the market is being invited into the most intimate corners of our lives.

The implications of this open invitation to a market invasion of health care cannot be ignored. Market theory posits a world of disconnected, hostile, adversarial actors guided by a winner take all ethic that reduces life to a series of exercises in competitive gamesmanship. In the marketplace, we must remember, the ruling motto is caveat emptor, let the buyer beware. In battles of the competitive marketplace, this corporate gamesmanship does not posit a new age win/win scenario, but the very old scenario of winner take all. Does this world view, with its ethic and mission, have anything to do with the care of sick, vulnerable, aging or dying human beings? Can we rely on corporate dominated health care to protect patients? I think not. Which is why I believe we must together reaffirm the conviction that the health care system must care for all members of society, whether rich or poor, in a humane and careful manner. We must devote our efforts to keeping people healthy as long as possible, but we must insist that when people get sick, as we all ultimately do, quality care is the only bottom line which we will honor.

References

Anders, G. (1994, December 21). Money machines. *Wall Street Journal.* p. A1.

Baer, E. D. & Gordon, S. (1994). Money managers are unraveling the tapestry of nursing. *American Journal of Nursing. 94*(10):38–40.

Baer, E. D. & Gordon, S. (1994, December 28). The gender battle in nursing. *The Boston Globe.* Op Ed, p. 15.

Baer, E. D. & Gordon, S. (1995, April 10). Home health care is fraught with danger. *The Philadelphia Inquirer.* Commentary, p. A9.

Braveman, P., Schaaf, M., Egerter, S., Bennett, T., and Schecter, W. (1994). Insurance-related differences in the risk of ruptured appendix. *New England Journal of Medicine. 331* (7):444–9.

Brooten, D. , Kumar, S. , Brown, L. , Butts, P. , Finkler, S., Bakewell-Sachs, S., Gibbons, A., & Delivoria-Papadopoulos, M. (1986). A randomized clinical trial of early hospital discharge and home followup of very low birthweight infants. *New England Journal of Medicine. 315*: 934–9.

Brooten, D., Roncoli, M., Finkler, S., Arnold, L., Cohen, A., & Mennuti, M. (1994). A randomized trial of early hospital discharge and home followup of women having caesarian birth. *Obstetrics and Gynecology. 84* (5):832–8.

Burner, S. T. & Waldo, D. R. (1995). National health expenditures projections, 1994–2005. *Health Care Financing Review 16* (4):221–42.

Caplan, A. L. (1995a) *Moral Matters.* New York: John Wiley & Sons.

Caplan, A. L. (1995b). Straight talk about rationing. *Annals of Internal Medicine. 122* (10):795–6.

Caplan, A. L. (1994a). Can money and morality mix in medicine? *Academic Emergency Medicine. 1*:73–83.

Caplan, A. L. (1994b). The ethics of casting the first stone: Personal responsibility, rationing and transplants. *Alcoholism. 18* (2):219–221.

Caplan, A. L. (1992). *If I Were a Rich Man Could I Buy a Pancreas? And Other Essays on the Ethics of Health Care.* Bloomington, IN: University of Indiana Press.

Cerne, F. (1994, June 20). The fading stand-alone hospital. *Hospitals & Health Networks 68* (12): 28–33.

Commonwealth Fund Press Release. (1995, July 26). Commonwealth survey finds higher dissatisfaction with managed care plans. *BNA's Managed Care Reporter,* pp. 88–9.

Dallek, G. (1995). *Consumer Protections in State HMO Laws.* Los Angeles, CA: Center for Health Care Rights.

Feder, B. J. (1995, June 16). CareMark to pay $161 million in accord. *New York Times.* p. D2.

111

Finkelstein, R. (1995). *The Managed Care Consumers' Bill of Rights: A Health Policy Guide for Consumer Advocates.* Albany, NY: Public Policy and Education Fund of New York, in cooperation with the Citizens Fund.

Fisher, A. quoted in Stachniewicz, S. A. & Axelrod, J. K. (1978). *The Double Frill* (p. 32). Philadelphia: Stickley.

Gordon, S. & Baer, E. D. (1994, December 6). Fewer nurses to answer the buzzer. *The New York Times.* Op Ed, p. 23.

Gordon, S. & Baer, E. D. (1995, January 24). Managed care, unmanaged pain: Keeping quiet on the 'tough choices.' *Angeles Times.* Op Ed, p. B7.

Gordon, S. (1995, February 13). Is there a nurse in the house? *The Nation, 260* (6):199–202.

Himmelstein, D. U., & Woolhandler, S. (1994). *The National Health Program Book: A Source Guide for Advocates.* Monroe, ME: Common Courage Press.

Hellander, I., Moloo, J., Himmelstein, D., Woolhandler, S. & Wolfe, S. (1995). The growing epidemic of uninsurance: New data on the health insurance coverage of Americans. *The International Journal of Health Services, 25* (3):377–92.

Institute of Medicine; Division of Health Care Services; Committee to Design a Strategy for Quality Review and Assurance in Medicare. (1990). In K. N. Lohr, (Ed.) *Quality Assurance.* Washington, D. C.: National Academy Press.

Institute of Medicine. (1986). *Improving the Quality of Care in Nursing Homes.* Washington, DC: National Academy Press.

Leape, L. L. & Brennan, T. A. (1991). The nature of adverse events in hospitalized patients: Results of the Harvard medical practice study II. *New England Journal of Medicine, 324* (6):377–84.

Lutz, S. & Pallarito, K. (1995, October 23). Not for profits stash the cash. *Modern Health Care, 25* (43):40–4.

National Health Council. (1995). *Putting Patients First* [Pamphlet]. Washington, D. C.: Author.

Nightingale, F. (1859). *Notes on Hospitals* (Preface). London: John W. Parker & Son.

Okun, A. (1975). *Equity and Efficiency: The Big Tradeoff.* Washington, D C: Brookings.

Pellegrino, E. D. (1985). The caring ethic: The relation of physician to patient. In A. Bishop and J. Scudder (Eds.), *Caring, Curing, Coping — Nurse Physician Patient Relationships.* Birmingham, AL: University of Alabama Press.

Riley, G. F., Potosky, A. L., Lubiz, J. D., & Brown, M. L. (1994). Stage of cancer at diagnosis for Medicare HMO and fee-for-service enrollees. *American Journal of Public Health, 84* (10):1598–1604.

Robert Wood Johnson Foundation Press Release. (1995, June 28). Sick people in managed care have difficulty getting services and treatment, new survey reports. (Study author is R. Blendon.) New Jersey: Author.

Shortell, S. M. , Morrison, E. M., & Friedman, B. (1990). *Strategic Choices for America's Hospitals: Managing Change in Turbulent Times.* San Francisco, CA: Jossey-Bass.

Shortell, S. M., Kaluzny, A. D., & Associates. (1994). *Health Care Management: organization. Design. and Behavior* (3rd ed.). Albany, NY: Delmar.

Stewart, A. & Ware, J. E, Jr. (Eds.). (1992). *Measuring Functioning and Well-Being: The Medical Outcomes Study Approach.* Durham, N. C.: Duke University Press.

SUPPORT Principal Investigators. (1995). A controlled trial to improve care for seriously ill hospitalized patients: The study to understand prognoses and preferences for outcomes and risks of treatment (SUPPORT). *Journal of the American Medical Association, 275*:1591–8.

Index

115

Springer Publishing Company

Total Quality Management in Human Service Organizations NEW
Toward the 21st Century
John Gunther, DSW and Frank Hawkins, DSW

The total quality management (TQM) paradigm presents a unique opportunity for human service professionals to break away from traditional management approaches. In this useful supplemental text, the authors provide a clear overview of the tenets of TQM, as well as illustrative and extremely detailed case studies in an array of human service settings, including health care, public welfare, and educational. The authors include two useful chapters on the emerging practices of benchmarking and reengineering. This text supplies the reader with a brief guide on how to implement TQM, as well as a useful glossary of terms for management students.

TOTAL QUALITY MANAGEMENT IN HUMAN SERVICE ORGANIZATIONS

John Gunther
Frank Hawkins

SPRINGER PUBLISHING COMPANY

Partial Contents:

Overview of Total Quality Management. Total Quality Management and Human Service Organizations • Total Quality Management: A Model of Implementation • The Tools of Total Quality Management

Applied Total Quality Management in Human Service Organizations. Health Care. The St. Joseph's Health Center Story • Freeport Hospital Health Care Village • Public Welfare • "Quality Oklahoma" and the Oklahoma Department of Human Services

Emerging Practices. Benchmarking • Reengineering • Epilogue

Appendix A: Total Quality Management in Human Service Organizations: A Guide to Implementation • Appendix B: State of Oklahoma, Executive Order 92.3 • Appendix C: "Quality Oklahoma" Strategic Plan • Appendix D: A Brief History of "Quality Oklahoma"

1996   264pp   0-8261-9340-4   *hard $40.95 (outside US $45.80)*

536 Broadway, New York, NY 10012-3955 • (212) 431-4370 • Fax (212) 941-7842

Springer Publishing Company

EXPERTISE IN NURSING PRACTICE
NEW

Caring, Clinical Judgment, and Ethics

Patricia Benner, RN, PhD, FAAN, **Christine A. Tanner,**
RN, PhD, FAAN, **Catherine A. Chesla,** RN, DNSc
Contributions by **Hubert L. Dreyfus,** PhD
Stuart E. Dreyfus, PhD and **Jane Rubin,** PhD

Based on the internationally renowned authors' major new research study, this book analyzes the nature of clinical knowledge and judgment.

The authors interviewed and observed the practice of 130 hospital nurses, mainly in critical care, over a six year period. The authors collected hundreds of clinical narratives from which they refined and deepened their explanation of the stages of clinical skill acquisition and the components of expert practice. The text underscores the practical implications for nursing education and administration.

**_xpertise
in Nursing
Practice**

Caring, Clinical Judgment,
and Ethics

■■■■■■■■■■■■■■■■■■■

Patricia A. Benner
Christine A. Tanner
Catherine A. Chesla

Partial Contents:

Introduction. Clinical Judgement. The Relationship of Theory and Practice in the Acquisition of Skill • Entering the Field: Advanced Beginner Practice • The Competent Stage: A Time of Analysis, Planning and Confrontation • Proficiency: A Transition to Expertise • Expert Practice

The Social Embeddedness of Knowledge. The Primacy of Caring, the Role of Expertise, Narrative and Community in Clinical and Ethical Expertise • The Nurse-Physician Relationship: Negotiating Clinical Knowledge Implications for Nursing Administration and Practice

1996   424pp   0-8261-8700-5 hard $46.95 (outside US $52.50)

536 Broadway, New York, NY 10012-3955 • (212) 431-4370 • Fax (212) 941-7842